10-8-04

To: Ann...

"SIR, YES SIR"

U.S. Marine Corps Boot Camp, Parris Island, South Carolina

Martin Iacampo, Sr.

Dear Baby doll
I love you very much
and I am very proud
of all of your
accomplishments

VANTAGE PRESS
New York

Keep up the good
work
Love
lm

In memory of Bernard (Big Ben) Iacampo, Sr.

Though this book is nonfiction, the names of many of the characters have been changed, to protect both the innocent and the guilty.

Copyright © 1994 by Martin Iacampo, Sr.

Published by Vantage Press, Inc.
516 West 34th Street, New York, New York 10001

Library of Congress Catalog Card No.: 93-94219

0 9 8 7 6 5 4 3 2 1

Printed in the United States by Morris Publishing
3212 East Highway 30
Kearney, NE 68847
1-800-650-7888

Contents

Acknowledgments   v

1.	How It All Started	1
2.	Signing My Life Away	3
3.	Making the Move	6
4.	The Arrival	9
5.	Meeting the Man (Staff Sergeant Grant)	13
6.	Processing	17
7.	The Barracks	26
8.	The Marine Corps Way	32
9.	The Green Wienie	52
10.	Getting Down to Business	57
11.	Characters	67
12.	Still in Our Faces	74
13.	The Pride of the Corps (DIs)	79
14.	Slack Was Coming	86
15.	The Smoking Lamp	89
16.	A Marine's Only Friend	93
17.	Breaking the Monotony	98
18.	I Still Didn't Learn	100
19.	Junk on the Bunk	102
20.	The Other Troops	105
21.	Looking Better	117
22.	Guard Duty	122
23.	Daily Activities	125
24.	Confidence Course	129

25. The Rifle Range 133
26. Mess Duty 140
27. Almost There 142
28. Elliott's Beach 145
29. Final Field 148
30. Dress Uniform Issue 149
31. The Final Touches 151
32. The Final Chapter 153

Acknowledgements

I want to give a very special thanks to my devoted wife and best friend Marianne Aiello Iacampo who has been with me through thick and thin. I would also like to acknowledge my children, Martin Iacampo Jr. and Monica Iacampo. Without the three of them my life would be incomplete.

Chapter 1

How It All Started

The train hadn't even come to a stop when I heard some commotion coming from the platform outside the train. I glanced out the window and saw this enraged person running up and down the outside of the train yelling his head off. I thought maybe the guy had just cracked up all of a sudden. I couldn't imagine what his problem was. I really had enjoyed the train ride to Parris Island very much, but now out of a clear blue sky emerged this nut who seems to have flipped his lid.

He was a lanky-looking hillbilly, with a pronounced southern accent and a mouth that ran a mile a minute.

"Hurry, get your asses off the train, put out those cigarettes, and spit that gum out of your mouths!" He kept shouting the same thing over and over, as if this whole scene was being played over and over again. "Hurry, ladies, get your asses off the train!"

My first impression of this nut was of a small person with a uniform who had some authority and was misusing it to the hilt. I had no idea that there were hundreds of him in this place called PI, Paradise Island, otherwise known as Parris Island, and only later would I find out he was one of the saner individuals.

"Hurry, get into ranks; spit that gum out of your mouths. Get your asses off the train. Let's go, ladies; we don't have all day."

Some of the newcomers that weren't moving fast enough

1

to suit this wacko were literally being pulled off the train. Little did we know that the word *ladies* that he used for us was going to be one of the nicer things we were going to be called for a good long while.

I began to wonder what had happened to the nice guys in dress blues in the recruiting office in Cleveland. They were nothing like this guy.

Chapter 2
Signing My Life Away

The date was November 11, 1958. I was seventeen years old today, and I couldn't get down to the recruiting office so I could get away from all this turmoil I was living under.

My father and I hadn't gotten along from the time I was born. I could never figure out what the problem was between us. My older brother, Benny, and I got knocked around like a couple of punching bags. I think the old man was taking his frustrations out on us. He was no slouch in the pugilistic sense; he was a very tough person. He was six-three in his heyday and could pack a good punch and wasn't afraid of anyone. He just had something against my brother and me and never gave us any slack. Getting whacked around by him when I was growing up gave me a really bad attitude, and I feared no one. That became a problem for me later on in life.

I can't entirely fault the old man for my joining the service, though, I had wanted to since I could remember. My relationship with him just helped me make up my mind more easily.

November 11 was a national holiday, not because of my birth, but because it was Veterans Day. The recruiting office was closed, so I couldn't go enlist that day. *What a coincidence,* I thought. *My birthday was Veterans Day, and I'm joining the Marine Corps.* I should have been born on the Fourth of July, and maybe I would have blown my head off with an M-80 instead of what I was about to do. I just couldn't wait to get down to the recruiter's office and sign on the dotted line.

On November 12, bright and early, I was standing in front of the recruiting office in downtown Cleveland, Ohio, with my mother at my side. I think she came down to make sure I didn't change my mind. She couldn't stand the way Big Ben and I didn't get along. This was a day I had anticipated for a long time.

The office was filled with many other kids my age preparing to enlist. I wondered what some of their motives were, if they had the same kind of living environment I did. At that time, the minimum enlistment was for four years. How stupid a person is when he is young.

The recruiters were very impressive in their dress blues. They looked just like the posters we used to see around trying to entice young men to join the Corps. *I can't wait until I look like one of those guys,* I thought to myself. Unfortunately, I didn't find out until it was too late that these guys were not any better than a used-car salesman trying to sell you a reconditioned piece of junk he had just polished up the night before. They would tell any lie they could think of to get a naive kid to enlist in the Corps. They did their jobs well. They were so convincing with their sales pitch, I thought I was enlisting for four years of travel, romance, and adventure, like the French Foreign Legion. One of the things they neglected to tell me was that the only thing I would be sleeping with for the next few months was an M-1 rifle.

At the recruiting office, one of the good old boys in dress blues asked me how soon I wanted to leave for Parris Island.

I said, "As soon as possible."

He said, "How about tomorrow?"

"Not that fast," I replied. "I have people I have to say good-bye to."

The departure date was set for November 17.

4

I had a lot of good friends while I was growing up. They were mostly Italian, but not all of them. All of them did come from good old-world-type families and were very generous people. They all extended dinner invitations to me, and I didn't refuse one.

At all of the places I used to hang around people were buying me drinks like I was going to World War II. In those days, everyone drank at a young age. I didn't refuse any drinks either. It was quite a distinction in those days to be a marine, and I was accepting all of the accolades. This whole thing was starting off better than I ever expected. I was getting a hero's send-off, and hadn't done anything yet.

Chapter 3
Making the Move

On November 17, the recruiters were noticeably different. All of the guys who had signed us up must have had twin brothers with rotten dispositions. These weren't the same group of guys I had met five days before. The party was now over. We recruits had made the big mistake of signing on the dotted line; now we were property of the U.S. Marine Corps. It was no longer necessary to cater to us youngsters; we had bought the car and found out it was a lemon and were stuck with it. The used-car salesmen had pulled off another snow job.

The mass confusion of military life was now under way. Move here; move there. Sign this; sign that. Don't do this; don't do that. Hurry up and wait. The changes in the recruiters' personalities were incredible.

When all of the last-minute details were taken care of, we recruits were ushered out of the building and into the street like a herd of cattle, then down to the train terminal.

I was always a sharp-looking kid. My appearance was always impeccable, and today was no different. I had on my best brown-checkered suit, which was very fashionable for the time, with a white shirt and tie. I was very anxious to get away.

Both of my parents were waiting at the train station to see me off. I couldn't tell what was on the old man's mind; he just gave me his usual look. I could tell my mother was slightly moved by my leaving but knew it was the best thing, due to the circumstances. We exchanged a few words. I kissed my mother good-bye and shook hands with the old man; then I got on the train with a big smile on my face. I don't know if the old man wanted to get a little more sentimental or not. I remember when I was about three years old I had gone to kiss him good night and he had slapped me in the face. He said men shook hands—they didn't kiss. From that day on, I never kissed him again.

I was leaving behind my older brother, Benny Jr., my younger sister, Celia, and two younger brothers, Mike and Tony. Mike and Tony were quite a bit younger than the rest of us. They were fourteen and sixteen years younger than I, respectively. They didn't have the same relationship with our parents that we older ones did. My father had mellowed by the time they were born. My younger sister, Celia, also had a different relationship with him than Benny and I did. She used to cry when I was getting the shit kicked out of me. I still can't to this day figure out what motivates people to hit their kids. A spanking sometimes is good, but a beating is a lot different. It was not uncommon in the forties and fifties to raise kids with ass whippings, although I sure never condoned it. In most old-world-type families, the father was the boss and was never challenged, and the Italians were certainly no exception.

Being number two, I always had to try harder. I still can remember running after my brother Benny with my pants falling off, trying to hang around with him and his friends. Even the kids I hung around with were slightly older than I was, and I was constantly getting slapped around. I was constantly getting beaten from all angles. All of the abuse I was taking was sure making a nasty person out of me. One thing for sure; I could take a punch.

Things didn't start off for me too well on November 11, 1941, the day I was born. I was four weeks old before they could think of a name for me. What a chore. My mother wanted me to be named after her father, Tony, and the old man wanted me to be Carmine after his father. I would have settled for either name, but as usual, Antoinette and Benny couldn't agree. The nurses and doctors in the hospital were calling me "boy" like I was in a Tarzan movie or something. Little did I know somewhere down the road I was going to be called boy thousands of times, but not with the same significance.

God bless my little grandmother Cecelia (my mother's mother). She finally interceded. She told my mother, "Antoinette, you'd better name that baby something; he is four weeks old already." To simplify things, my mother looked at the Catholic calendar and saw that November 11 was Saint Martin's day, and that was the name of that tune. It's a good thing I wasn't born on Saint Felix's Day.

Here I was, seventeen years later, sitting on a train in Yesmasse, South Carolina, home of the U.S. Marine Corps boot camp, Parris Island, having some raving jerk running up and down the platform, ranting and carrying on, calling us all ladies and screaming for us to get off the train. I hadn't had three days' peace since I was hatched.

"Get into ranks; spit that gum out of your mouths," he kept repeating with that annoying southern drawl. No one knew what the hell ranks were, but he kept yelling for us to get into them. Was it possible that everyone here was as nasty as this big-mouthed person, or was he just having a bad day? It wasn't too long before we found out that he was one of the more timid people that we would run into.

Finally he got everyone into what he was calling ranks and started ushering us down the street to a place called the receiving barracks. The procession resembled a bunch of cattle being herded to the slaughterhouse.

Chapter 4
The Arrival

When the cattle drive eventually reached its destination, the receiving barracks, we were rudely ushered into a room that resembled a large sun porch. In the room were a lot of neatly made bunks. This place was set up to receive recruits, accumulating enough people to form a platoon. People were coming from all parts of the country, ten and twenty at a time. It took approximately eighty recruits to form a platoon. I was very impressed with the cleanliness of the barracks, being a clean freak myself. Everything was polished from top to bottom.

Cleanliness was not the order of the day for some of my future comrades. Some of them looked like they hadn't seen the rain room for months, and had the body odor to go with it. I would have thought that they would have taken a shower before coming to PI. Although things were a little rough in the harmony department in my family, cleanliness was a top priority.

The first night we spent in the receiving barracks I lay in my bunk reflecting on the good time I had had coming down on the train to Parris Island. I was always a friendly person and made friends easily; on the other hand, I had a knack for making enemies also.

At one of the stops the train made, a girl got on, and naturally I struck up a conversation with her. When she told me that she was going to Parris Island, I asked her whom she was going to see. She informed me that she had joined the Corps and was going to PI as a recruit. I was sort of surprised, because I didn't know that the Marine Corps had women in their ranks. What a pleasant surprise! I always had a thing for women. Things were looking up now. She told me that her boyfriend was in the Corps and she had joined in order to see him. That was true love, I thought. The recruiter that signed her up must have been a cousin to the guy in Cleveland. The possibility of her being stationed near her boyfriend was very remote. Another snow job from the used-car salesman.

It seemed like the train made a stop every couple of hours and picked up more recruits. It was taking a long time to get to PI, but I was enjoying myself. What a way to go! No one yelling at me, meeting new people, and getting a free train ride. Little did I know this free train ride was going to cost a lot more than I had bargained for.

Once again the train stopped, and this big fat kid got on board. I could tell he was Italian because of the way he looked and acted. After all, I was born and raised on East 110th and Woodland in Cleveland. If you never went out of the neighborhood, you never knew that anything but Italian people existed, so I could pick an Italian out of a crowd easily. He seemed to be a very nice person. Unbeknownst to him at the time, he was in for a rough time at PI. I was like the welcoming committee for everyone that got on the train. The Italian kid and I started to have a nice conversation. This was great.

Paul Paul was a tall, skinny kid that got on the train somewhere down south. It didn't take too long to notice that there was something drastically wrong with this guy. He was a real wacko. To start, his parents must have been as nutty as he was because of the obvious: his name. I would think that they could have been a little more creative naming him. They were trying to dump him off on Uncle Sam. For the rest of the way to PI he was entertaining everyone by sticking a straight pin through his finger joints and through his cheeks. Everyone was laughing their heads off at this nut, and he loved it. Hell, this was really getting good. Free entertainment, too.

As only a good Italian mother could do, my mother had packed me a going-away lunch to beat all lunches. Eating is a big thing in the true Italian home. Although I weighed only 150 pounds when I joined the marines. I always ate like I was going to prison. In the package was one of my favorite foods, fried chicken, some cheese, fresh bread, and some other goodies. I was soon eating the chicken and throwing the bones out the train window. What could be better? Meeting people, eating chicken, getting entertained, and getting away from the hassles at home. Boy, I was sure looking forward to getting to boot camp.

We stayed at the receiving barracks for two or three days, until there were enough people to form a platoon. We spent our time telling jokes, lying around, and sizing each other up, which was the normal macho thing to do. Little cliques began to develop. The black guys were on one side of the room, the Italians and other ethnics were on the other, and in the corners were some of the boys from the hills, who had a distinctive look about them. There was no animosity among anyone; we were just sizing each other up. Mostly everyone was talking to everyone else, but there were a few who thought they were bad actors among the crowd.

Our only obligations at the time were to make our bunks and keep the barracks clean. We ate three meals a day. The food wouldn't win any awards, but it was palatable. From what I had observed to this point, boot camp wasn't too difficult at all. With the exception of the wacko that had met us at the train, it seemed pretty normal to me. I thought I had made the right decision in joining the marines. Throughout our stay at the receiving barracks, Paul Paul kept us in stitches with his pin tricks.

For the most part everyone was getting a little restless waiting for our training to start. We all knew that what we were doing was not what boot camp was all about, and we were getting antsy.

I had heard some war stories from different people, about how tough Marine Corps boot camp was, but I thought everyone always made things sound a lot harder than they really were. All of the stories combined couldn't have prepared me for what was about to come. On November 21, 1958, D day finally came. If I had a crystal ball, I would have gone over the hill then and there.

Chapter 5

Meeting the Man (Staff Sergeant Grant)

In the lower level of the receiving barracks was a room set up with a lot of desks like a classroom. We were ushered down the steps and into this room by the guy that had met us at the train. He had two stripes on his sleeves, and by now we had found out that he was a corporal. We had gotten used to his screaming by now; the few times we saw him, we just thought he had a big mouth. The desks were very neatly lined up, and the room was, like the rest of the barracks, very clean.

I was not really paying too much attention, but I saw, as well as everyone else, two guys standing in front of the room. The smaller of the two looked to be half-normal, but the bigger guy, at first glance, looked like he had a chip on his shoulder for the whole world. He was the most intimidating person I had ever seen.

The two guys stood in front of the room like statues and didn't make a move. The corporal was running his mouth off again. "Hurry, ladies; you'd better find a seat and get your ass in it." Both of the guys standing next to him had completely shaved heads, from what we could see, as they both had on these Smokey the Bear hats. (In the Corps they are called campaign hats.) The smaller of the two had one more stripe on his sleeves than the corporal did, and the mean-looking one had one more than the little guy did. Both of them were very sharp-looking in their uniforms, but the little guy looked more squared away. He was spit and polish from head to toe.

The mean-looking guy was sharp-looking but looked like he had just come off a binge, and he probably had. His face was full of pockmarks. It looked like his face had caught on fire and someone had put out the fire with an ice pick. For added intimidation, they both had their pistol holsters open, each with a mean-looking weapon exposed. My mind started to work a mile a minute. Were these guys our drill instructors? God forbid. If they were, I'd rather be locked up with Jack the Ripper.

The corporal yelled out, "Listen up, ladies! The first thing you are going to learn here at Parris Island is that when you are spoken to, you will answer only one of two ways! Sir, yes sir, or sir, no sir! Now keep the racket down and get into your seats! Quit milling around" (one of the many terms we would have to get used to). After everyone was seated, which didn't take too long, he continued. As he stood in between the two guys he said, "This man on my right is Staff Sergeant Grant, who is going to be your senior drill instructor. The man on my left is Buck Sergeant Bail; he is going to be your junior drill instructor. From this day on until you graduate from Parris Island, if you do, these two men are going to take complete control of your lives. They will be with you twenty-four hours a day. They are going to be your mother, your father, and your constant supervisor. You will not make a move unless they tell you to. If they tell you to shit, you had better squat and ask what color they want." I thought, *Boy, things are sure heating up now.* "They will be with you day and night. You will not make a move unless they tell you to. It is their unpleasant mission to try and make United States Marines out of you, if that is possible." The corporal was really acting nuttier than he had before, putting on a show for these two frightening-looking guys. "Some of you will make it through boot camp, but most of you won't. If you are one of the lucky ones, you will have earned it."

If the two DIs were trying to intimidate us, they were doing a good job. Neither one of them uttered a word up to this point. They just stood there with their hands on their hips and glared at everyone.

Everyone was taking in what the corporal was saying; then out of nowhere the mean-looking guy yelled at the top of his lungs, with a voice only a savage could possess, "GET THE FUCK OUTSIDE!" Sheer terror went through everyone. We flew out of our chairs like rockets, headed for the doorway. All of a sudden, there were eighty people trying to get through a standard-sized doorway at one time. "You bunch of shit birds, you better get the fuck outside and get into formation! Hurry! Hurry!" People were literally trampling one another trying to get through that door. The effect this guy had on us in a matter of minutes was incredible. Everyone was punching and clawing one another trying to get through the door. It resembled a riot at a rugby match.

Both of the DIs were screaming obscenities by the dozens. Every once in a while one of them kicked someone in the ass for good measure. "What the fuck is the matter with you shitheads? When I tell you to get outside, that is what I mean. You'd better hurry your goddamn asses up!" I couldn't figure what the hell was going on; this was insanity.

Eventually everyone made it through the doors and into the street, but only after tearing the doors off the hinges.

The screaming was relentless: "Get the fuck into ranks! Keep your eyes straight ahead! Who the fuck are you looking at, boy? You'd better never eyeball me, boy! Do you hear me, boy? You'd better never eyeball me, boy, or I'll kick your fuckin' ass! Do you hear me, boy?"

Sergeant Grant was running up and down trying to get everyone into position, acting like a demon was in him.

Sergeant Bail was adding to the confusion but was not as boisterous as his boss. "Get your shoulders back and your chin

15

tucked in, boy! What the fuck is the matter with you? Can't you hear me? You must be deaf, boy! Can't you hear me?" He was getting into everyone's face as much as he could. He was so enraged that he was foaming from the mouth while he was screaming, "Pull that stomach in! You look like a fat fuckin' pig, boy, and we don't allow pigs in my Corps! Who the fuck are you looking at boy? I told you never to look at me, didn't I, boy? I'm gonna rip your fuckin' eyeballs out and skull-fuck you, boy, if you keep lookin' at me!"

All the while this craziness continued they were pushing us back and forth, getting us into formation (columns and lines).

"You'd better not move when you are in formation. Do you hear me, boy? You never move while you're in ranks. Is that clear? What the fuck are you moving for, boy? I told you never to move in ranks. Are you a dumb motherfucker? Did your mother send you to me because you are a dumb motherfucker and can't understand English? Now get your ass squared away."

I couldn't believe all of this. What the hell was going on? I felt like I was in a concentration camp. These two guys must have been from a different world. People I knew didn't act like they did, and I knew plenty of nuts. Any normal person would have passed out from all that yelling.

Chapter 6

Processing

With everyone completely confused and disoriented, the DIs began to herd (in boot camp you are herded everywhere you go until you learn to march) us up and down the different streets on our way to the processing center, all the while pushing, shoving, and screaming. The confusion was too much to believe. I thought I was having a nightmare. I was ready to go home and get a civilized ass whipping, which I was used to. Everyone was stumbling over one another, stepping on the heels of the person in front of them. It was complete pandemonium and chaos.

"Stay in formation. Quit looking around. Keep your eyes straight ahead. Didn't I tell you never to look at me, boy? You shit birds better start listening, or so help me, I'll kill you."

At this point I believed this madman. Besides the fact that I was scared to death, and I wasn't one to get scared easily, I said to myself, *I can't believe I joined the Marine Corps for four years. I haven't been here for three days and can't take this. I didn't know how lucky I was at home. I wonder if I should try and run away tonight? No, I'd better not try that. If I don't make it, they might kill me.* I never in all my dreams of being in the military ever expected anything like this.

When the herd finally arrived at the processing center, the yelling and turmoil was continued at a frantic pace by both DIs. But the little one, Sergeant Bail, couldn't hold a candle to Sergeant Grant. Every once in a while a slap or kick came out of nowhere to let you know they were still there, like the screaming wasn't enough. I didn't know if I was the only one on the receiving end of the blows, and I was too scared to look around.

First on the agenda was stripping off all our civvies (civilian clothing) and putting it in a box. We had been instructed by the used-car salesman before leaving home not to bring too many personal belongings with us, because we wouldn't need them. All the while our newly appointed chaperons were stalking us throughout the process.

Next on the list was getting a haircut, if that is what you want to call it. I stood and watched in horror while the kids in front of me were being sheared like sheep at cutting time. I was always so particular about the way my hair looked, and I wasn't ready for this.

When it was my turn, I got into the chair, and this goddamn sadist they called a barber began running the clippers over my scalp, and with each pass he took off a half a pound of skin. I thought that Orlando's Barbershop, on Woodland, had some rough barbers.

All of these bastards must have gone to the same shearing school, as every recruit soon looked the same. The haircuts looked like the pictures I saw of concentration camps in World War II at the Regent movie theater on 116th and Buckeye. All of the barbers were civilians employed by the government. They must have gotten paid by the number of cuts they gave, as they would crank out a haircut in under three minutes. The gouges in everyone's necks and heads were very apparent. I thought I might need stitches. It took me half my life to get my hair the way I wanted it, and it took them thirty seconds to destroy it. It was hard to believe. I could barely recognize any of the other recruits after the haircuts.

When the shearing was completed, we were all crammed into a large shower room and told to scrub down. As I said before, some of the recruits were really ripe. We scrubbed from head to toe. I ran my hands over my head while showering and felt the absence of my locks. This place was a nightmare.

Next was a visual inspection by some guy they called a doctor. He could have been a milkman for all I knew. He checked our noses, throats, ears, underarms, and, last but not least, our rectums.

One of the recruits was so shook up at this point that when he was told to bend over and spread his cheeks, he spread the cheeks of his mouth instead. Anyone who noticed it was too afraid to laugh.

All this time the two newly appointed guards were trying to keep everyone in line by their yelling and screaming: "Okay, ladies, keep the fuckin' lines moving! Keep your asses squared away! Hurry up, ladies! We don't have all day! Get the rags out of your asses, girls! Move it! Move it."

I didn't find out until much later that the DIs didn't overdo the abusive language and the physical abuse outside of their private areas. It was no secret that the abuse did take place, but it was supposed to be kept under wraps. As long as no one was sent to the hospital or had any broken bones, everything was in order. Until one of the DIs was caught beating someone, and that rarely happened, all was kept quiet. If they were caught, they were busted and reassigned off Parris Island.

Being issued clothing was next on the agenda. We were issued everything from head to toe. The issue started with socks, skivvies (underwear), covers (hats), pants, and shirts. The last items to be issued were our shoes and boots. Sizes didn't mean too much. As long as it was within a half-size, you got it, and when I say "you got it," I mean they threw it at you.

There was a platform constructed where the recruits

went up one side, got fitted, and then went down the other side.

Issuing the footgear was a person in a marine uniform, but I didn't know what rank he was. But that really didn't matter. At Parris Island, all recruits address anyone that isn't a recruit as sir. Anyone that wasn't a recruit had to be treated like God by the recruits.

It was my turn to be fitted for footwear. I was standing on the top of the platform when the marine that was fitting the shoes started to harass me about where I was from. Then he called me boy. I hated that expression, but I found I had better get used to it and a lot of other names.

Using my Cleveland logic, I figured this guy wasn't my DI, so why did I have to take any shit from him? I answered him like I would someone back home when I got challenged: "Who the fuck do you think you're talking to?"

At that point he yelled over to Sergeant Grant, who wasn't far away. "Hey, Sarge, we have a guy over here that thinks he's a badass!"

Without hesitation, Sergeant Grant made his way over to the platform where I was standing. The marine shoe salesman I had mouthed off to repeated to the good sergeant what I had said. With a look in his eyes that could kill a person, Sergeant Grant reached up and grabbed me by my newly issued shirt and pulled me off the platform. I wound up in a standing position right in front of Sergeant Grant, who still had me by the shirt. I was shitting in my pants. We were inches apart, nose to nose and toes to toes. I never had known when to keep my big mouth shut; it had been a problem all my life. This time I knew I was in deep trouble.

"Boy, you're one of the wise motherfuckers from up north that thinks you're gonna come down here and do whatever you want, aren't you, boy?"

"Sir, no sir," I responded.

Sergeant Grant was so mad he was spraying saliva from his mouth when he was yelling. "Boy, I like wise motherfuckers like you down here, cause I know how to deal with you shit birds." He was introducing me to an entirely new vocabulary, Marine Corps style.

"What's your name, boy?"

"Private Iacampo," I replied, "sir."

"Private Yacambho, you will only speak when spoken to, and you will only answer, 'Sir, yes sir,' or 'Sir, no sir.' Do you understand me, private?"

"Sir, yes sir."

"From here on in, until you graduate from my island, and I will do my best to see you don't, my Marine Corps doesn't like wise motherfuckers; you have had the green wienie. I'm gonna fuck with you in ways you never thought of. I'm gonna teach you to keep your big fuckin' mouth shut if it kills you, and it might."

His face was as red a fire engine, and his veins were sticking out about two inches. Obviously, I didn't know what the green wienie was, but I was very sure I was going to find out.

"Now get the fuck back in line. I'll deal with you later."

"Sir, yes sir."

The last pieces of gear issued were our seabags. We crammed everything that we had been issued into them and waited for our next command. (Nothing in Parris Island is done without a command.)

Next we were herded to another large room where some doctor gave us a mass eye examination. As long as you could see the chart, you passed the test.

(Most people don't know the Marine Corps is a department of the navy, and all of its professional personnel, such as doctors, nurses, and corpsmen [male nurses], are only attached to the Corps. Although they wear Marine Corps uniforms in some cases, you can tell they are in the navy because of their insignias.)

When the eye exam was completed, we were all sitting on the floor. We were all asked if we had any illnesses that were missed in our exams. If there were, we were to raise our hands. The wheels began turning in my head. Now this was a good chance to get myself out of this mess. I raised my hand.

After acknowledging some other recruits, the doctor called on me. I was really desperate.

"What is your problem, son?"

Those were the kindest words spoken to me all day; here was my chance to get out of the mess I was in.

I got off the floor and said in a humble voice, "Sir, I have a bad case of athlete's foot." It was the only thing I could think of. The doctor did everything he could to keep from laughing his head off.

As for Sergeant Grant, I think that pissed him off even more at me, thinking that some snot-nosed kid was trying to get out of his beloved Corps with athlete's foot.

To this day I still laugh at myself, thinking that I was that desperate to use this lethal illness to try to get out of the marines.

The last thing on the agenda was the dental exam. The navy officer that examined us must have gone to the same school as the barbers; he was brutal. He wedged everyone's mouth open and did his exploratory with a tool that looked like an ice pick. He was not a gentle person or a credit to his profession. He jabbed and probed with the tool he was using and called code numbers to some stooge with a clipboard. I believe that the dentist, as well as others at Parris Island, didn't want to be stationed there any more than we wanted to be there and were taking their frustrations out on the recruits.

With our newly issued seabags slung over our shoulders,

we were given our next command in the manner we had better get accustomed to.

"Okay, ladies, let's hurry and get out into the street in formation. We don't have all fuckin' day. Let's see if you assholes remember what the fuck a formation is. Hurry. Hurry."

It must have been a pathetic sight, eighty new recruits with new wrinkled uniforms on, covers pulled over their ears, new boots that didn't fit well, and, most of all, in a state of confusion.

"All right, girls, get in line. Keep the rows straight. Get into a good formation. Stand still and at attention when you are in formation, goddammit. I don't want you to move a fuckin' muscle when you are at attention," Sergeant Grant informed us.

After much confusion, all the recruits formed, as best we could, the formation. The next command was given by Sergeant Grant.

"Forward march. Halt."

With that command, everyone bumped into the person in front of them.

"Goddammit, when I say forward march, all of you shit birds start off with your left foot. Now let's try this again, ladies. Forward march."

There came a new added feature to our new language, called cadence. This was something the DI called out while we were marching to keep us in step with one another.

"Left, right, left, right, left!" Sergeant Grant called out as we marched. "You definitely are the sorriest bunch of maggots I have ever seen. Get it together, ladies. When I say left, your left foot is supposed to hit the ground; when I say right, your right foot is supposed to hit the ground. Jesus H. Christ, what the fuck is the matter with you assholes? You'd best get in step before I run all you maggots in the swamp."

Singling out one of the recruits, Sergeant Grant started, "Private, don't you know your left from your right? You have to be one of the dumbest motherfuckers that ever came through these gates. You'd better get into step, boy, or I'll rip your arm off and beat you with it. Is that clear, boy?"

"Sir, yes sir," the young recruit responded.

Sergeant Grant kept up his tirade. "How many times do I have to tell you girls which is your left and which is your right? All of you assholes get down and give me fifty push-ups."

Here we were in the middle of the street, with our seabags draped over our shoulders, doing push-ups (the most common form of nonviolent punishment given in boot camp; with no exaggeration, if I didn't do twenty thousand push-ups while at PI, I didn't do one).

The push-ups were grueling. Not only because of the physical aspect, but because the asphalt pavement was very hot and burned our hands. All the while we were struggling with the push-ups, we were doing them to the count of Sergeant Grant. Every time the count got to ten or fifteen, he started all over again. Fifty push-ups turned out to be 150.

"Okay, girls, we can do these push-ups all fuckin' day. When you do a push-up your chest is supposed to touch the ground. Now let's get them right. Get your dead asses off the ground and let's try it again, ladies.

"Left, right, left, right. Goddammit, platoon halt. I shouldn't call you bunch of sick-lookin' assholes a platoon. Everyone put your left hand on the ground. Now step on it; I said step on it. Now do you know which is your left? And the other one, for your fuckin' information, is your right. Now when I say forward march, step out with the foot that you just stepped on your hand with. Is that clear? Is it?"

"Sir, yes sir!"

How in God's name could anyone yell as much as this guy

without falling over dead? If I could have expedited his demise, I sure would have.

After about two dozen attempts, four hundred push-ups, and seventeen "motherfuckers," the herd finally made it to our new USO (a home away from home).

Chapter 7

The Barracks

The barracks was of wooden construction. It was a two-story building, probably built during World War I. Four squad bays comprised one set of barracks. One squad bay was above the other, on two different sides of the building. In between the squad bays were the heads (toilets and showers). Directly opposite the heads were the DIs' quarters.

As we were standing at attention in front of the barracks, Sergeant Grant started another dissertation.

"If you fuckin' maggots live through your basic training, which is thirteen weeks, this is the place where you are going to collapse every night after I run your asses all over this island, and run you will. You will never walk anywhere on my island. Everywhere you go you will either march or run; you will never walk. Is that understood?"

"Sir, yes sir."

"You bunch of sick-lookin' vermin are going to be known as Platoon 2028. You do not deserve to be called a platoon, but we have to call you something. You will be billeted on the second floor, right hand side, of this building you are in front of. When I give the command, you will get your dead asses up these steps on the double—remember we never walk anywhere—and get in front of one of the racks in the squad bay. You will stand at attention in front of one of the racks until Sergeant Bail and I assign you your bunks. Now get the fuck up there."

With the same fury we had left the receiving barracks with, all eighty recruits ran full force toward the doorway. This time the entrance seemed smaller, because we all had our seabags over our shoulders. The results were even worse than before. The sight of all this had to look like sheer panic. The pushing and shoving must have resembled rush hour in the New York subway, only magnified one thousand times. All the while Sergeant Grant was yelling and screaming. This bastard must have eaten gunpowder for his meals, judging by the way he acted.

Sergeant Grant was standing at the doorway kicking people in the ass and ranting, and Sergeant Bail had gone ahead and was at the top of the stairs, doing his part to keep the herd moving.

"You ladies better hurry and get your asses up these steps; we don't have all fuckin' day. Move it. Move it."

When the last survivor finally made it up the steps and to the squad bay, we were all wandering around like lost sheep. There wasn't one recruit among us that wasn't totally confused, frustrated, and scared.

"How many times do I have to repeat myself, goddammit. Get in front of one of the bunks and stand at attention. When you stand at attention, your hands are at your sides with your thumbs facing outward, your shoulders are back and straight, your fuckin' guts are pulled in, your chin is tucked in, eyes are straight, and you do not under any circumstances move one muscle in the mess you call a body. Last but not least, you will never talk to anyone, only the drill instructor, when you are talked to. No talking to anyone. Is that clear?"

"Sir, yes sir."

The milling around finally subsided when everyone found a rack to stand in front of.

"We have many rules and regulations in the Marine Corps, and the first is one: you never under any circumstances

27

wear your cover indoors. For your information, a cover is the hat all of you maggots have on your heads. When you come indoors, you will tuck your cover in your belts in the front of you and in the center of your body. Is that clear?"

"Sir, yes sir."

"The only assholes that wear their cover indoors are the fuckin' people in the army and air force. The only time you will wear your cover indoors is if you are on guard duty and are armed, God help me. Now get those fuckin' covers off and give me fifty push-ups."

Again the fifty turned into one hundred.

"When your name is called you will answer loud and clear. Is that clear?"

"Sir, yes sir."

"Upon answering your name, I will assign you a rack. You will always answer in a loud, clear voice. You will run to the assigned rack on the double, and I mean run. You will stand at attention in front of that rack until you are given further orders. Your rack is meant for sleeping and nothing else. You will not ever sit on your rack, or put anything on your rack without permission. Is that understood."

"Sir, yes sir."

"I can't hear you girls; you'd better speak louder. Get down for push-ups."

Everyone screamed at the top of their lungs, "Sir, yes sir!"

The state of mind everyone was in reminded me of a bunch of robots that had just come off the production line and not yet been fine-tuned. No one knew where they were going or what they were doing. Everyone was just trying to follow these insane orders to the best of their ability.

As each name was called, the respective recruit answered and literally ran to his assigned bunk. A couple of recruits forgot to answer because of the confusion. Everyone had to do push-ups.

"You fuckin' ladies will learn that when one of you fucks up, you all get punished. You are a platoon, or supposed to be a platoon, and a platoon works together. When one fucks up, you all pay the price. You shit birds are gonna get squared away if I have to kill all of you."

God only knows, everyone believed him.

Sergeant Grant didn't have too much of a problem with the American names, although he was no scholar. When he got to the ethnic names, he really butchered them, especially the Italian names, which were few. I don't think that there were too many Italian people in Mississippi where he came from.

"Yacambo, Eacambo. How the fuck to you pronounce this fuckin' name?"

"Sir, Iacampo, sir," I answered.

"Private Yacambo, you're the wise motherfucker at the receiving barracks, aren't you."

I had no idea what to say, so I answered, "Sir, yes sir."

"Well, Yacambo, I got a lot in store for you, boy; now get the fuck in front of the rack I assigned you."

"Sir, yes sir."

After the rack assignment was completed, I was in such a state of shock and confusion I didn't even recognize the person that shared the bunk with me. I had the top rack, and he had the bottom. He was the Italian kid I had met on the train on the way to PI. It was a combination of confusion and the haircut that threw me off, but mostly confusion.

With each bunk there were two footlockers. The person on the top rack had the locker in front of the rack, and the person on the bottom had the one that went under the bunk.

This was the way of Parris Island. Everything on the island had its place. In footlockers all of your belongings had a specific place. Clothing was placed in one area, toilet articles in another, writing paper in another. If you went into any barracks on the island, every footlocker would look the same. The Marine Corps way, or no way.

Sergeant Grant in his eloquent manner began to explain the rules of the footlocker.

"Listen up, ladies. In the Marine Corps everything has its proper place, and that goes for your footlockers as well. There will never be anything thrown into your lockers. It will be placed in its proper place. If it isn't placed in its proper place the whole group of you shit birds will pay dearly. In all eighty footlockers your shaving cream, for some of you pussies that shave, will go in the same place, as well as your toothbrushes. Do you read me?"

"Sir, yes sir."

Sergeant Grant went on for twenty minutes, as we placed everything according to his direction. Sergeant Bail just paced up and down the squad bay, while Sergeant Grant screamed out all of his commands.

"If you do not follow orders while you are here at Parris Island, I will make sure that your stay here is not a pleasant one, and I don't expect to make it pleasant. This is not a country club, or some fuckin' resort. Some of you pussies may be used to fuckin' room service, and having your mothers wipe your goddamn asses, but, girls, you now are in the Marine Corps. You by a long shot are not marines; you have to earn that privilege. The only thing I'm gonna do for your ass is kick it. I have been assigned the unpleasant task of trying to shape you sick bunch of broads into marines. I have had similar assignments before, and I can tell you, half of you fuckers won't make it. You will do exactly what Sergeant Bail and I instruct you to do and nothing else. If you do not follow orders, I will make you wish you had never been hatched. You ladies signed up to be in my beloved Corps, and from this day forward, you'd better give your souls to God, because your fuckin' asses are mine."

"Sir, yes sir."

This guy didn't have any respect for anything; nothing was sacred to him—that is, nothing but the Corps. In the same sentence he used the name of God and referred to our "fuckin' asses." What a guy. I thought I was doomed to hell; all of this dialogue was in reference to our footlockers and belongings. Didn't this guy ever run out of air?

Chapter 8
The Marine Corps Way

DIs had many missions to accomplish with their new recruits. They attended lengthy schooling to develop certain training methods. Needless to say, most of them employed their own techniques after being a DI for a while. Some were more passive than others, but basically they had to possess the killer instinct in order to intimidate the recruits. Intimidation is a very big part in the training process. If a recruit is not intimidated by the DI, he will not follow his orders without reservation. Many times the senior DI, as in the case of Sergeant Grant, is the worse of the two and the junior DI just follows along as Sergeant Bail did. The thing that separated Sergeant Grant from the rest of the DIs was that he liked what he did and stepped way past his boundaries.

After the intimidation, they tried to break down the recruit mentally, so he would lose all of his former identity and his civilian ways. All activity from here on in was the Marine Corps way, or no way. You had to eat, sleep, and think like a marine in order to be considered a marine.

Strong-willed people like myself had a very hard way to go in boot camp. Some people had sense enough to keep their mouth shut and conform, but I was always a nonconformist. Not for long. The quieter, more reserved recruits went through boot camp with little or no beatings from the DIs.

Thinking for yourself in boot camp was taboo. We had to follow orders, whether they made sense to us or not, and without question. Making any decisions for yourself could be disastrous.

After the mental process was under way, the physical process began. It was the duty of the DIs to put their recruits in the best physical condition of their lives, by any means short of killing the person, and sometimes I thought they were trying to even do that. The complete recruit was someone that was in the best physical and mental condition of his life, followed orders without question, and was a killing machine.

Like Sergeant Grant, some of the other DIs were extremists in terms of their training methods. Some of them began to act like gods and thought they were gods, while doing some outrageous things only legal in boot camp, where they were supreme rulers.

One night, several months before I got to PI, one such DI came off liberty drunk and decided to take his platoon on a midnight run through the swamps that surrounded the island. After the run, three of his recruits didn't make it back to the barracks. In the search, they found the three recruits drowned in the swamps. That was probably the most severe case of abuse in Marine Corps boot camp history.

Sergeant Grant wasn't that bad, but he was a borderline case.

After we had placed all of our gear in our footlockers according to the Marine Corps manual, with Sergeant Grant's guidance, it was finally time to eat. I had a silly notion that while we were eating we would be able to enjoy our food and get away from the madness for a few minutes.

"When I give you ladies the word, you will get your delicate asses into the head and wash those filthy fuckin' hands and face. In my Marine Corps, we do not allow slobs in the mess hall. You girls don't have all day to wash, do you hear me?" Sergeant Grant stated.

"Sir, yes sir."

"When you are finished washing, you will get your lily white asses back outside in front of the barracks in formation. You don't have all day, ladies."

With that, there was a frantic rush to the head. There was plenty of pushing and shoving, with eight sinks and eighty people. No one wanted to be the last one out of the head.

The mad rush down the stairs was not quite as bad as the incoming trip, as some of the recruits were still in the head. At the top of the steps Sergeant Bail was ushering people down in the usual Corps manner—a boot here, a slap there. None of his aggression was done with malice, more out of duty and just going through the motions. He definitely did not have the mean streak that his boss did.

In the street was Sergeant Grant exercising his vocal cords.

"You ladies better get into ranks, and I mean on the double. We don't have all fuckin' day."

Confusion still existed as to where everyone should be in ranks.

"Cut that goddamn milling around when you are in formation. You are supposed to be standing at attention.

"I will now assign you to your position in ranks, and that will stay your position for the duration of your time in boot camp unless I tell you so. As I point to you, Sergeant Bail will place you where you belong. I hope for your sake you dumb fucks can remember your assigned positions. I hate repeating myself. Is that clear?"

"Sir, yes sir."

He sure could have fooled me about hating to repeat himself. I never heard anyone repeat himself so much in all my life.

As the recruits were on the way past him, he would slap

some of them in the back of the head, yelling for them to move out on the double.

"I thought I told you maggots when you are in ranks you will stand at attention. Get down and give me fifty."

Once everyone finally got to their correct position in ranks, the next command we heard was: "Left face." By that time, everyone was tired, hungry, annoyed, and still very confused, so everyone turned a different way.

"What the fuck is the matter with you shit birds? Don't you know your left from your right? How many times do we have to go over the same thing? Give me fifty."

Actually, not everyone was making the same mistake. Even with such a short time together, it was apparent that a few in the platoon were either very dense or just stupid. No one would be causing this chaos on purpose. But as Sergeant Grant said, if one fucked up, we all paid the price.

Singling out one recruit in particular, Sergeant Grant ran up to him. He was about six-six and looked like someone that had just came out of the hills for the first time.

"What the fuck is your name, Private?"

"Wayne, sir."

"Wayne what, you dumb fuck? General Wayne? Captain Wayne? Or is it Private Wayne?"

"Private Wayne, sir."

"This goes for all of you fuckin' idiots. From here on in, you do not have a first name. Your first name is Private. All of you fuckheads have the same first name: Private. Is that clear, Private Wayne?"

I couldn't see Wayne, but I could tell by the tone of his voice that he was scared shitless.

"Sir, yes sir."

"Now, Private Wayne, why is it that when I say left face, you turn the opposite way? Are you that fuckin' stupid?"

"Sir, I don't know, sir."

"Jesus H. Christ, Wayne, if you don't know why you are turning the wrong way, who the fuck does, huh, Private Wayne?

"Private Wayne, put your left hand on the ground. Now stomp on it. I said stomp on it, Wayne. Now can you remember which hand is your left and which is the right?"

"Sir, yes sir."

"Platoon, attention. Left face, right face, left, right, face."

Back and forth we went about two dozen times, until everyone got it right.

"Forward march. Platoon halt." Everyone bumped into the person in front of them. "Christ almighty, when I say forward march, you bunch of assholes should all step out with your left foot first. Give me fifty push-ups."

The death march continued all the way to the mess hall, with about ten different times when we had to stop and do push-ups because someone made a mistake. Thank God the mess hall wasn't far from the barracks.

I have never in my life done so many push-ups. I was physically and mentally exhausted.

By this time, I figured Sergeant Grant would have had a stroke or something from all his screaming. All of this insanity happened and we didn't even eat lunch yet. God, I hated the fact that I ever thought of going to the service. I should have been hit by a bus on the way to the recruiting office.

Everything I experienced so far at boot camp made me think of prisoners of war that were brainwashed by the enemy. But this was just the tip of the iceberg.

The new addition to our torture was standing at attention for thirty to fifty minutes without so much as wiggling our noses or blinking our eyes. To add to our discomfort, all this took place with two special enemies: the South Carolina sand flea and the boiling sun.

"When you ladies are standing at attention in front of the

mess hall or anywhere else, you will not move a muscle. You will keep your shoulders back, your guts pulled in, your chin up, and eyes straight ahead. I don't give a fuck if one of my sand fleas flies in your nose, your ears, or your eyes. You will not touch that sand flea. If any one of you ever kills one of my sand fleas, he will be brought up on murder charges. Is that clear?"

"Sir, yes sir."

"Who the fuck are you lookin' at, Private Asshole? I told you never to look at me, didn't I? If you look at me again, I'm gonna gouge out your fuckin' eyeballs. If any one of you shit birds ever looks at me, I will kick your ass all over this island. Is that clear? Do you read me?"

"Sir, yes sir."

Didn't this guy ever take a break?

As we stood at attention in front of the mess hall, the two wardens paced up and down the ranks, looking for someone to move. If they caught someone, the push-ups ensued. The yelling never stopped: "Boy, you'd better look straight ahead": "Boy, you'd best not move while at attention": "Boy, you'd better get squared away. If you want to keep those eyeballs in your head, boy, you'd best not look at me."

Just like it was rehearsed, a big black named Jackson swatted a sand flea that was pestering him. Sergeant Bail saw him.

"Sergeant Grant," Sergeant Bail called, "we have a murder on our hands!"

Sergeant Grant ran over to the scene of the crime as fast as he could and got into Jackson's ass with both feet.

"I just two minutes ago told you shit birds that if you killed one of my sand fleas you would be brought up on murder charges and, boy, you went ahead and killed one. What the fuck is your name, boy?"

"Private Jackson, sir."

"Private Jackson, do I have to talk in African for you to understand what I say? Do I, boy?"

"Sir, no sir," Jackson replied, in a shaky voice.

Sergeant Grant had to get up on his toes to get right in Jackson's face and was screaming his ass off.

"This sand flea happened to be one of my favorite sand fleas, and you went ahead and killed him. What the fuck is on your mind, boy?"

"I don't know, sir."

"This really pisses me off, boy. I am gonna put this flea in my pocket, and after chow I want you to report to me. Is that clear, Private Jackson?"

From where I was standing in ranks, I saw Sergeant Grant bend over and pick up something and put it in his pocket. Only God knew what it was, probably a piece of sand.

The rest of the platoon stood motionless for a long, long time. It seemed like two hours. It probably was only forty minutes or so. The hot sun was beating down on us, and our new natural enemies were doing a job on us. If a worse torture existed on the face of this earth, I didn't want to experience it. From time to time a slap was heard coming from someone's head that had moved.

The time finally came for Platoon 2028 to go into the mess hall.

"When I give you the command, you shit birds will go in single file into the mess hall. You will take a tray provided for you, and take what is given you to eat. Your mother is not here cooking special for some of you candyasses. You will sit where Sergeant Bail directs you to, and will not start to eat until I give the order. Do you read me?"

"Sir, yes sir."

As we filed into the mess hall, some of the recruits forgot to take off their covers. The madman was right there, ripping them off their heads, cussing them out, and throwing the covers at them. Soon everyone caught on.

Everyone went through the chow line like we were hypnotized, staring straight ahead, afraid to turn our heads. The people that were serving the food were slinging the food into our trays and making snide remarks. They seemed, like all the rest of the people we ran into at PI, nasty. I didn't find out until later on that these people were recruits, just like we were, that were on their last leg of boot camp. They were probably doing to us what others had done to them when they were greenhorns.

Sergeant Bail was directing us to our respective tables. Everyone sat down motionless until Sergeant Grant arrived.

"From here on in, ladies, you will sit and eat at attention. It will be done in the following manner. You will sit with your back straight, eyes forward. There will be no eyeballing in the mess hall. You will have your chin tucked in, and your shoulders back."

"Sir, yes sir."

"Your fork or spoon will come in a straight line from your tray to your mouth. It will then make an *L* shape into your face and then dump the food into that hole in your head. It will then come straight from your mouth in another *L* back down to your trays."

"Sir, yes sir."

"This method and only this method will be used when you are eating. The United States Marine Corps has paid good money to feed you shit birds. You will eat everything on your trays, and you will not spill any of the food on your uniforms. Keep your eyes straight ahead, your backs straight, and commence eating."

This was total madness. We couldn't even enjoy our food. I wished I were somewhere else.

It was virtually impossible to eat at attention without

getting food all over yourself. Mashed potatoes were easy, but the corn and peas were impossible to keep on your fork without looking down at what you were eating. When we were finished eating, it looked like everyone had been in a food fight. I have seen people without etiquette before in my life, but we all looked a mess when we were finished eating.

It seemed like we had just sat down to eat when the warden was already on our backs again.

"You ladies don't have all day to eat. Do you think that this is a restaurant, or do you think your mother is still waiting on you? Hurry up and eat. When you are finished, you will walk to the end of the mess hall and scrape your trays in the GI cans. There better not be any food left on your trays. You will then pile your trays at the scullery, then get outside in the same formation that you were in when we came to the mess hall. I want to see just how many of you shit birds remember what place you were in formation. Now hurry up and get outside."

While trying to hurry, some of the recruits put their covers back on while still in the mess hall.

"Jesus H. Christ, don't you shit birds hear when I tell you something? You never put your covers on indoors in the Marine Corps. You shit birds should have joined the fuckin' army, and I wouldn't have to put up with you dumb fucks. If I have to repeat myself again about those covers, I'll rip your fuckin' heads off and shit in them."

In all my life I had never seen anyone get worked up like this guy. His heart must have been made of stone. Any normal person would have had ten heart attacks already. And on he went.

"What the fuck is the matter with you shit birds? I have never in all my life seen a bigger bunch of pigs. You are supposed to put the food that my Marine Corps pays dearly for in your fuckin' mouths, not on your clothes. Not only did you fuck up your uniforms; you wasted good military money. You girls better get squared away. If you think you have problems now, you ain't seen nothing yet."

"You, Private." Sergeant Grant pointed to one of us. "Is that your position in ranks that I assigned you? Is it, boy? What the fuck is your name, boy?"

"Private Wayne, sir."

"What the fuck is that thing on your head between your ears called, boy?"

"My head, sir."

"You might call it your head, boy, but you don't have a fuckin' brain in it. If you did, you would have remembered your place in ranks. Isn't that right, boy?"

"Sir, yes sir."

"Now get down and give me thirty push-ups and see if that helps you to remember. I don't have all fuckin' day to repeat myself to shit birds like you, Wayne. The more I have to talk to you, the less time I have to get these other shitheads squared away.

"Attention. Right face. How many times do I have to tell you all to turn at once? You have to be the dumbest bunch of shit birds I have ever had. If you don't get squared away, you'll never make it through boot camp. Get down for push-ups.

"Right face, forward march. Goddamm it, I said to step out with your left foot first. I have a dog home smarter than you fuckin' turds.

"Private, how many feet do you have?" Sergeant Grant screamed at one of the recruits.

"Sir, two, sir."

"One is your right and the other is your left, isn't it, Private?"

"Sir, yes sir."

"Do you know which one is your left, boy?"

"Sir, yes sir."

41

"If you do, why in Christ's name did you step out with your right foot? If you maggots don't start listening to me, I'm gonna kick your asses all over this island. All of you, get down for push-ups."

By this time everyone's arms could barely support them, but the counting continued. Mostly everyone was exhausted to the maximum and just trying to go through the motions.

"Get on your feet, you bunch of pussies. Let's see if we can do it right this time.

"Attention, right face, forward march, left, right, left, right."

Amazingly, everyone did it right that time. I don't know if it was pure luck or some of those backwoods people were finally understanding what the program was. When the platoon finally made it back to the barracks, the command "Platoon halt" was given.

While we were still at attention, Sergeant Grant drilled us for about twenty minutes, left face, right face, about-face. In between, several hundred push-ups were done.

"When you girls are dismissed, you will get back upstairs in the squad bay in front of your racks and stand at attention. Private Jackson, you will remain here at attention. I have some unfinished business with you, boy! Now the rest of you shit birds fall out and get your asses in the squad bay. Dismissed."

The platoon didn't witness what happened between Sergeant Grant and Jackson. We were told that the sergeant made Jackson dig a six-by-six hole with an entrenching tool and bury the alleged dead sand flea. After the hole was completely dug, Sergeant Grant reached into his pocket and threw something into the excavation. Jackson said it could have been a piece of lint for all he knew. Then Jackson backfilled the hole he had dug. Sometime during this process Sergeant Bail went down to oversee Jackson and Sergeant Grant returned to the squad.

Before the rest of the platoon was standing in front of the

racks at attention. Sergeant Bail was pacing up and down the squad bay, trying to act as tough as Sergeant Grant. As afraid as everyone was, I think they all had Sergeant Bail's number. He just wasn't the vicious person Sergeant Grant was.

"You girls have three minutes to wash your hands and faces. We don't like any cruds in the Marine Corps. You will wash your faces and brush your teeth after every meal. I can see by the looks of some of you girls you are allergic to soap and water. We are going to change that. I never want to smell an odor coming from anyone of you. It is your responsibility as a platoon to see that everyone keeps themselves in good order. In the Marine Corps, we work as a team. If one of you is dirty, that means the rest of you are dirty. If one of you fucks up, you all will have fucked up. When you leave the head area, I expect it to be as clean as it was when you went in there. You will make sure the water is turned off and the sinks are wiped. When you use the urinals, make sure you don't piss on the floor. You are not at home anymore. Most of all, you'd better never shit on the toilet seat. If I ever catch anyone shitting on the toilet or pissing on the floor, I will wipe your goddamn nose in it. Do you read me?"

"Sir, yes sir."

All the while the lecture went on, Sergeant Bail paced up and down the squad bay. This was the most we had heard from him. Usually, Sergeant Grant made all the noise. He was still outside attending to Private Jackson.

"Now get the fuck in the head and clean up. Move it; move it."

While we were in the head cleaning, Sergeant Bail and Sergeant Grant made a switch. Sergeant Bail was keeping an eye on Jackson, and Sergeant Grant came up to the squad bay to take over the indoor harassment.

I had, as well as the rest of the recruits, witnessed and experienced brainwashing firsthand. In just a short amount of time these two DIs, primarily Sergeant Grant, had all eighty people jumping through hoops at will. By now we were so demoralized we would have jumped off a building if they told us to. I was considering that anyway. The beginning stages of boot camp were the most critical as far as the Marine Corps was concerned. All the rules and regulations were thrown at you in the first few days. The transition from civilian life to the Corps way was very drastic. I don't care where you came from or how tough you thought you were; you either conformed, got your ass kicked, or were thrown out of the Corps. There were no exceptions. I saw guys that thought they were really tough become pussycats in no time. The DIs were very professional at their work, especially Staff Sergeant Grant. He loved his job.

"Hurry, ladies; you don't have all day to scrub your faces. Hurry and get back in front of your racks. Who in the fuck left the water running in the head? Everyone get down and give me fifty push-ups."

While we were doing the push-ups, between counting Sergeant Grant went into another tirade. "You shit birds were told never to leave the water running by Sergeant Bail. You girls must have shit between your ears. I don't know what the fuck I have to do to make you listen.

"Get in front of your bunks and stand at attention. It's now time for you girls to learn what bunk drill is all about. You will do exactly as I say, and when I say it. Get on your bunks; get under your bunks; get behind your bunks; get over your bunks."

He was calling out these orders so fast that no one could understand his commands. There were bodies flying all over the place. There were mattresses and linen strewn all over, and the commands kept coming. This had to resemble an unorganized tumbling act in the circus, only pathetic. Everyone was bumping into everyone else. Bumps and bruises were

44

common from collisions. To make matters worse, in all the confusion some of the foot lockers were tipped over and their contents were on the floor. The tumbling act lasted for five minutes.

"Get back in front of your racks. You shit birds have ten minutes to get this squad bay back in order. If it's not in order in ten minutes, you'll wish you were never born. Now get with it."

Under normal conditions, it would have taken an hour to straighten this mess out. There was no way in the world we could do it in ten minutes. Here again, we were given the impossible to do, as a part of the breaking down process continued.

"Let's get with it, ladies. We don't have all fuckin' week to get this squad bay back in order. You got eight minutes left."

It was complete pandemonium. Everyone was tripping and falling over each other to try to get their own equipment back into their footlockers and get their bunks back in order. When ten minutes or so elapsed, the push-ups began, lasting for ten more minutes. I never thought that the human body could endure all of this abuse.

It took quite some time to get the squad bay straightened out. After it was, we were given the order to fall outside in front of the barracks again.

For the next two hours we did a multiple combination of left face, right face, about-face, and marching drills. In the interim, we did hundreds of push-ups. The pavement was still as hot as it was before. I was shocked no one had blisters on their hands from the heat. As I said, in the public view, the most Sergeant Grant did was slap someone in the back of the head or kick him in the butt. He kept his serious pounding restricted to the barracks.

"It'll be a long time before you girls even begin to look like marines. You are an insult to humanity. You are lower than whale shit. I have never in all my Marine Corps career seen such a bunch of shit birds. I don't think there is a word to describe you turds. Now get the fuck at attention and stay that way until I give you further orders.

"When you are dismissed, you will fall out and get up to the squad on the double and wash up for supper. I don't know why the Marine Corps would waste food on you bunch of shit birds. You will wash up and get your fuckin' asses back down here in formation for chow. You have exactly three minutes. When I say on the double, I mean on the double. You never walk anywhere on my island. Is that clear."

"Sir, yes sir."

"Fall out."

"Sir, yes sir."

The DIs had such a system of moving people and being in three places at once, it was incredible. No sooner did Sergeant Grant dismiss us than it seemed he was in the squad bay screaming at the top of his lungs at us. How the hell could this guy be in so many places at one time? Maybe there were two of these lunatics? It couldn't be.

With an enormous amount of pushing and shoving, everyone got back in the street in formation. To my surprise, everyone was in the right formation. But sure enough, something had to be wrong.

"That head looks like a bunch of fuckin' pigs were just in there. The only place pigs belong is on the ground. Now get down for push-ups."

I wasn't paying much attention, for fear of my life. No one would dare look around, but this was the first time I had seen Jackson since the flea funeral. With a quick glance, I could tell he was exhausted from the detail. He was soaked from head to toe with perspiration.

"If Private Jackson's example wasn't good enough for you shitheads, I will again make it perfectly clear. Anyone that is

46

caught killing one of my sand fleas will be punished severely. And I will catch you, won't I, Private Jackson?"

"Sir, yes sir."

On the way to the mess hall we had half of the problems we had before. We only stopped four times for push-ups.

Again we stood in front of the mess at attention, with our newly found enemies harassing us. I didn't think that all this effort was worth the meal. All the time we stood there, our masters paced up and down the ranks yelling their heads off. Percentagewise, Sergeant Grant made 95 percent of all the noise. Sergeant Bail just followed along with the program.

In the chow hall, we received the same excellent service we got before, as all the food was thrown at us. We ate at attention, with the same result as before, food all over us. This time everyone removed their covers when entering the mess hall and put them back on on the way out.

The march back to the barracks was similar to the prior marches, a Chinese fire drill, with one exception. As small as it seemed, there was a slight improvement; people were starting to catch onto the marching routine. It was not extremely noticeable, but just a glimmer of hope aroused in me.

"When you maggots get the word to fall out, you will do so on the double, get up to the squad bay, and stand at attention in front of your bunks. Fall out."

Still terrified, everyone made their way for the doorway on the double. By now there weren't any doors hanging. If anyone had pushed me like that in civilian life there would have been a battle. Here at PI, everyone was just trying to survive.

Once I got into a fight with some kid in front of the Park Pharmacy (a drug store) on 110th and Woodland in Cleveland because I got shoved. It was nothing like how I was getting pushed around now. All of these little things kept coming into my head. I was sure better off at home. The two Jewish guys that owned the drugstore, Sid and Milt, came out and broke up the fight. It was amazing how the Jews and Italians got along in those days. Home wasn't too bad after all.

In the barracks, in front of our racks, at attention, Sergeant Grant began.

"This is going to be your home for the next thirteen weeks, if you make it. This squad bay will be kept in immaculate condition. I can't stand slobs. I will not have any slobs in my platoon. In single file, you girls will pass by the deep sink where Sergeant Bail will issue you a pail, a bar of soap, a towel, and a scrub brush. While at the deep sink, you will fill your pail with water. This pail and scrub brush will remain in your possession until you leave this island. You will leave this island one way or another. Either by graduating or in a pine box. You will be issued this gear only once. The Marine Corps's only issues gear one time. If you lose this gear, you will answer directly to me. Now move out in single file.

"You ladies are now going to learn how to scrub the floors, Marine Corps style. You will all be responsible for your areas around your bunks. The head will be cleaned three times daily by assignment. The correct way to scrub the floor is in a clockwise fashion. You will not use too much soap or water; I do not want my floors to warp. When the scrubbing is completed in your areas, you will remove the excess water from the floor with your towel and wring it out in the pail you were issued. This will be done once a day. You are not at home anymore, girls, where your mother wipes your ass for you."

We were all directed to our assigned areas in the typical boot camp manner and began the floor-scrubbing ritual. I had no idea what we were scrubbing; the floor was cleaner than any house I was ever in.

"You'd better not get any of the soap and water on my shoes," Sergeant Grant said as he walked up and down the squad bay. "If you get water on my shoes, boy, you'll be up all night shining them," he remarked to one of the recruits. "Did your mama wipe your ass for you when you were home, boy?"

The recruit answered while still kneeling on the floor, "Sir, no sir."

"You had best stand at attention when you talk to me, shit bird. You never talk to me if you're not at attention."

The recruit jumped up and stood at attention directly in front of Sergeant Grant. "Sir, yes sir."

"Didn't I tell you never to look at me, boy? Why the fuck are you staring at me, huh, boy?"

"I don't know, sir."

"You don't know, Private. Who in the fuck does know? Get down and give me fifty good push-ups. You had better never look at me again, Private. Is that clear?"

"Sir, yes sir."

When the floor scrubbing was completed, we filed by the deep sink, emptied the water, and returned to the front of our racks.

"You cruds are now going to take a shower. You will take a shower every night before hitting the rack. I will not have any filthy-ass recruits in my platoon. You will take a shower by the numbers in the following manner. You will turn the water on and wet your dead asses down, then turn it off. You will then soap yourself and wash every inch of your fucked-up bodies. You will then turn the water back on and rinse off. You will not waste any of the Marine Corps water. When you are finished with your shower, you will then dry off and put on clean skivvies. You will then return to the front of your racks, stand at attention, and wait for further instructions. If I smell the least odor coming from one of you pigs, you will all pay the price. There will be no sleeping in the raw. The only people that sleep in the raw are fuckin' queers. The Marine Corps has no tolerance for queers. Are any of you queers?"

"Sir, no sir."

"There will be ten of you at a time that shower. The rest of you shit birds will stand at attention in front of your racks until it is your turn."

All the while the showers were being taken, Sergeant Grant stood in the doorway yelling to hurry and shut off the water.

Showers were taken in record time, and then everyone stood in front of their bunks at attention.

"As I look down the squad bay I see a lot of you pussies have your undershirts tucked in your underpants. In the Marine Corps, we do not tuck our undershirts in our underpants. It is not acceptable. If your shirt is tucked in your pants and you have crabs, when you pull off your shirt you will get crabs in your eyebrows. Now all of you assholes that tucked your shirts in your pants, get them the fuck out. Who the fuck are you lookin' at, boy? I told you never to look at me. Get down and give me fifty.

"When the order to hit the rack is given, you will hit the rack immediately. You will lay as still as a fallen tree. There will be no talking or moving around. You will not move a muscle; you will lay perfectly still. I don't even want to hear you breathe. You will not get out of the rack for anything whatsoever. If you have to piss, you'd best drink it. There will be no getting up. Is that clear?"

"Sir, yes sir."

"Now hit the rack."

Everyone was so completely physically and mentally exhausted, this was a welcome command. Everyone dove into their racks.

This was the best news all day. Maybe when I woke up I would find this was a bad dream. I had a sick feeling come over me. This was only the first day; I had thirteen weeks of boot camp ahead of me. I had been in some tough spots in my life, but this was the absolute worst. Why did I listen to my old man and those so-called friends of mine that told me to join the marines? It sure was nice getting that hero's send-off, with all those free drinks and dinners. But if I had known this, I sure would have never signed up.

When my head hit the pillow, I thought, *At last some peace and quiet.* You could hear a pin drop in the barracks. Finally I could get some sleep and maybe this nightmare would go away. As I began to pass out from exhaustion, I heard a blood-curdling scream come from the middle of the squad bay, coming from Sergeant Grant: "PRIVATE YACAMBO, REPORT TO MY QUARTERS AT ONCE!" My heart almost stopped from fright.

"Sir, yes sir," I answered. I levitated myself right out of the rack and flew down the squad bay. What in God's name does this guy want now? I couldn't even go to sleep in peace.

Chapter 9

The Green Wienie

Sergeant Grant's room was about one-quarter of the way down the hall on the left side. Through all the day's activities, I had forgotten all about the episode with the marine shoe salesman in the processing center.

I stood in front of Sergeant Grant's doorway and said, "Did you call me, sir?"

"Private Yacambo, that is not the way you report to me. You will do it in the following manner. [I knew he wasn't pronouncing my name the right way, but I was not about to correct him.] First and most important, Private, you will never look at me. Do you see those eyeballs pasted on the window?"

"Sir, yes sir."

"When you address me you will look at those eyeballs and never look directly at me."

"Sir, yes sir."

"Next, Private Yacambo, you will report to me in the following manner. You will stand at the side of my hatch, pound on my hatch so I can hear you, and you will announce yourself: 'Sir, Private Yacambo is reporting as ordered, sir.' When I acknowledge you, you will take one step forward, make a left face, and center yourself on my hatch. You will never look at me; you will keep your eyes on those eyeballs. Now, get back there and report to me properly."

"Sir, yes sir."

All of this communication took place at very close quarters. I had thought this guy was mean-looking and ugly before, but after a long hard day, he looked twice as bad. By the looks of him, I'd say he was a stone juice head (alcoholic).

Following his orders, I stood on the left side of his doorway and pounded I thought very hard and said, "Sir, Private Iacampo is reporting as ordered, sir."

"I can't hear you, boy. You'd better hit that pine harder."

Again I hit the door frame and announced myself. Again he said he couldn't hear me.

"I don't want to keep this up all night, boy. I have to get some sleep. You'd better hit that pine so I can hear you."

This went on about three or four more times, until he finally acknowledged me.

"Front and center."

I stepped front and center and did a left face as I had been instructed. By this time my knuckles were bleeding from beating the door frame, and I didn't even notice it.

"You'd better keep your eyes on those eyeballs, boy."

I had no idea what was coming.

"Private Yacambo, you're one of those wise motherfuckers from up north that thinks you can come into my Marine Corps and do and say anything you want, aren't you, boy?"

"Sir, no sir."

"Well, boy, we like wise motherfuckers like you down here, cause we know how to deal with that kind."

Out of nowhere came a shot to my solar plexus that knocked me to the floor and almost knocked me out. I was lying on the floor gasping for air with Sergeant Grant standing over me.

"Get on your feet, boy."

I think he was surprised he hadn't knocked me out.

"Private, you're gonna learn that here on Parris Island you are only gonna speak when spoken to and only answer when asked to. Is that clear, Private Yacambo? Boy, you have just got what I call the green wienie. You'd better never fuck with me again, or I'll kick your ass all over the base. Every night that I am on duty you will report to me in the same manner. The nights I am not on duty you will report to my junior drill instructor, Sergeant Bail. With Sergeant Bail you will do calisthenics for one half hour with this dumbbell."

He pointed to an iron pipe that had a coffee can on each end filled with concrete, a homemade dumbbell.

"Now get on your feet, Private. You're bleeding all over my fuckin' floor."

He handed me a paper towel he got from his room for me to wipe the blood off the deck. He wasn't concerned about my bleeding hand; it was the floor he was concerned with.

"Now get your fuckin' ass back in the squad bay, and hit the rack. If I hear a sound out of you, Yacambo, you will pay dearly for it."

I flew down the hallway as fast as I could.

The sergeant really hadn't hurt me that bad; he basically just knocked the wind out of me. But if I let on that he hadn't hurt me, he really would have beaten me.

As I lay on the rack, I couldn't believe that I had jumped from the frying pan into the fire. Here I was in a worse situation than I had been in at home. At least after I took a beating from the old man I could go off and lick my wounds. Here I couldn't hide anywhere. My ass was really in a jam.

As I lay in the rack, I remembered a particular day when I was younger and at home. It was a beautiful summer day, and the yearly feast was being put together at Latin Field, on 116th and Woodstock. This was the highlight of the year for all of the kids in Mount Carmel Parish. Latin Field was a place where all of the DPs (displaced persons from Europe) held their soccer matches. All the kids in the neighborhood used to hang around there, smoking and having fun. One time my father caught me and my cousin Pete smoking there and kicked us in the asses all the way back home.

The feast had all kinds of rides, prizes, games, and food. The biggest hit in the food department was the Italian sausage sandwiches. As Mount Carmel was a Catholic church, the people that attended the feast could eat meat on Friday, as long as it was at the feast. (In those days, eating meat on Friday was against the Catholic church's rules.) In the name of profit for the church, it was okay.

All of the kids used to break their necks to get to the feast and help put up the rides and stands. Those that did help got free rides opening night. I was always the first one there.

Being that I was the only one in the family that wasn't afraid of heights, I was always elected to pick the cherries in the tree behind our house. On the first day of the feast, Big Ben decided he wanted me to go up the cherry tree and pick him some cherries so he could bottle them in wine. While he and my brother Benny Jr. waited on the ground, I scooted up the tree, and in my haste I was ripping the cherries off instead of picking them. The difference was that the stems were pulled off of most of them, and that was not good for bottling. I filled the basket as soon as I could, so I could go to Latin Field. When I got on the ground, with the basket of improperly picked cherries, the old man went nuts, just like he had so many times before. He punched the shit out of me, all over the backyard, threw me against the house, and was clawing at me like a caged lion. Although I had been defiant to the old boy, I had never talked back to him. This time I was sick and tired of being used for a punching bag, and I stood up to him. I told him if he ever put his goddamn hands on me anymore, he would never see me again. That was the last time he hit me.

So here I was at PI, lying on my rack, with Godzilla right down the hall, wondering if I had been better off at home. The answer for now was yes. The last thing that entered my mind before I passed out that night was if I hadn't taken so many beatings from the old man, I could have never handled this situation with my surrogate father in boot camp.

Chapter 10

Getting Down to Business

This was the worst night's sleep I had had in all my young life. Aside from all the mental and physical torture I had gone through that day, I had a bloody, swollen hand from beating on Sergeant Grant's door frame. I'm sure that all of my fellow recruits also had had one of their worst days.

It seemed like we slept for about twenty minutes when this maniac Sergeant Bail came running through the squad bay beating on everyone's rack with an iron pipe and screaming. God almighty; it wasn't a nightmare; I was still here at PI. God knows what time it was but it was still dark outside.

"Okay, ladies, drop your cocks and grab your socks. Get the fuck out of those racks. You aren't at a fuckin' resort."

Then Sergeant Grant started. "Let's get with it, shit birds; we don't sleep till noon here. You're in the Marine Corps now."

Everyone was still in a state of shock from the day before and walking around, bumping into each other.

"You ladies have only thirty seconds to hit the head and get on your uniforms and get in front of your bunks at attention. You will put on everything except your covers."

People were falling over trying to put on their boots, their socks, and the rest of their uniforms.

"Let's get with it, ladies; get in front of your racks.

"When you get the word, you will all fall outside behind the barracks in formation. We are going to see what kind of shape you assholes are in. At Parris Island, we never walk anywhere; we run. We either run or march. Rain or shine, it doesn't matter. Get outside."

Each time we went up and down the stairs we did it with a few fewer casualties. When we got outside, Sergeant Grant was waiting for us; this guy must have had a twin. It seemed like he was always in two places at one time. He looked liked a lion tamer, waiting to crack the whip.

"Which one of you shit birds pissed on the floor in the head? I told you if one of you fucks up, everyone pays. Get down for push-ups. One-two-three-four-five-six, you ladies better straighten up; we can do these all day. Keep your backs straight, arms shoulder width apart, and touch your chest to the ground. Seven-eight-nine-ten-eleven."

The highest he ever counted was to fifteen; then he started over. Maybe he couldn't count higher. We had to do a hundred push-ups. Needless to say, a lot of recruits were in very poor physical condition. They were huffing and puffing.

"We're gonna shape you lardasses up if it kills you, five-six-seven-eight-nine-ten. Keep them going, girls."

From my standpoint, there was nothing I could see that was positive about boot camp. I'd been beaten up, been scalped, had the green wienie, eaten at attention, spilled food all over myself, almost broke my hand punching some nut's door frame, been cussed at, been slapped in the head a dozen times, stood at attention for hours to eat some garbage food, and had sand fleas fly up my nose, in my ears, and in my eyes, and now I was out here on the parade field at four o'clock in the morning, if that was what time it was, doing push-ups because some dumb hillbilly pissed on the floor. If only I had had a crystal ball, I wouldn't be in this mess.

"What the fuck is the matter with you, Private Wayne? You still don't know where your position in ranks is? What's the matter with you, boy? Are you lost? You're so fuckin' dumb you can't remember one minute to the next. You should have brought your mother to boot camp with you, boy, so she could wipe your dead ass for you. You look like a lost sheep, lookin' for the flock. You'd best get the cobwebs out of your head and get with the program. A good marine always knows where he is. You wouldn't make a pimple on a good marine's ass. If you don't get squared away, I'm gonna stick this size eleven so far up your ass it will come out of your mouth."

I had heard people bust balls before in my life, but this guy had to be the world's champion. He came up with things and sayings I never heard of.

"We start all of our morning PT [physical training] with jumping jacks. We do everything on my island by the numbers. I count and you jump. Do you read me?"

"Sir, yes sir."

"Now let's get it together, girls. One-two-three-four-five-six-seven."

We must have done two hundred jumping jacks. After the jumping jacks the command was given: "Platoon, halt."

"Right face, forward march, double-time march. Let's keep it together, girls. Left, right, left, right. You are the sickest bunch of maggots I have been stuck with. I'm gonna get your asses in shape or kill you trying. Left, right, left, right."

I had always kept myself in pretty good shape, but I was not prepared for this. I don't think anyone could prepare for this. On this first morning run we hadn't gone more than one-eighth of a mile before people were falling out by the numbers. While they were falling out the DIs were kicking them in the ass and screaming at them, "You girls remind me of a bunch of pussies! My wife is in better shape than you are! You shit birds better get used to this running, cause there is a lot more of it to come! You maggots that can make it better drag these other shit birds along! You are in the Marine Corps now and will act as a team!"

The strong always have to help the weak. That was not my cup of tea. I have always fended for myself; now I had to stop and pull along some out-of-shape person that I barely knew. To make matters worse, half of the guys were throwing up. What a life.

Ninety-nine percent of the DIs were in good physical condition. (Their mental state was questionable.) Not only did they count cadence while running with the platoon; they used to run backward, calling cadence, and keep up with everyone. But their condition depended a lot on how much they had drunk the night before. Mostly all of them liked their booze.

It was too early in our training for the DIs to know our individual names, with the exception of a few, like Wayne, Jackson and me, who were introduced under much less than pleasant circumstances, so they just pointed, screamed, and made gestures to the people they wanted to address.

After about a quarter of a mile, the platoon made a U-turn. More than three-quarters of the recruits were dragging their asses as we were headed back to the barracks. Throughout the run the two sergeants' mouths had never stopped: "Keep it together, ladies; keep it together. I'm gonna run you out-of-shape assholes in the ground. You bunch of pussies are gonna get into shape, or you will wish you never came to my island." They took the words right out of my mouth.

Back behind the barracks we did about two hundred push-ups in the typical manner, Sergeant Grant never counting past fifteen.

"We can do these push-ups all fuckin' day, ladies; you'd better get them together."

On several occasions, the good sergeant made reference to *we*. *We* can do this and *we* can do that. From where I stood, *we,* the dummies, were the only ones doing anything. I found that rather amusing. It wasn't much to laugh about at the time, but it helped.

"Okay, ladies, get on your feet. You mass of out-of-shape turds make me want to puke. When I give the order, you will fall out, get up to the squad bay, and square it away. After your racks are made up, you will hit the head and clean up before chow. You will wash your faces and clean that crud off your teeth. You will have ten minutes to do this. I mean ten, not eleven, not twelve, ten minutes. I have no idea why my beloved Marine Corps wants to spend good money to feed you shit birds. You'd better move your asses; we don't have all fuckin' day."

I thought I grew up with people with bad mouths, but they all seemed like altar boys next to Sergeant Grant. He used words and sayings I had never heard of.

Everyone was going nuts, trying to get their areas squared away and get in and out of the head.

Picking one of the recruits, Sergeant Grant started, "Boy, I thought I told you not to talk to anyone unless you got permission. There will be no talking to anyone at any time, or I'll sew your fuckin' lips together. Do you read me, boy?

"Hurry, get the rags out of your asses and get down into formation in front of the barracks."

With all of the pushing and shoving, I would have thought people would be getting mad at one another. But no one was getting pissed off. There really wasn't any hostility between the recruits at this point; everyone was just trying to survive.

But there were a few times Jackson and I collided with each other, and a few dirty looks were exchanged. Neither one of us was used to being pushed around, especially by someone other than a DI. I could always sense when there was a problem coming, I could tell somewhere down the road the big black kid and I would lock horns.

For about the next three days the tempo didn't stop. We didn't get a minute's rest. My brains were scrambled constantly. The DIs were doing a job on us. The only good thing about this whole scenario was that time was passing quickly. There wasn't a clock anywhere, but through all the harassment mealtimes came very rapidly. That was my only means of gauging time.

Once again we were in front of the barracks, in formation, but the commands weren't as confusing as before. It seemed that even the less intelligent recruits were catching onto the procedures.

I never realized before coming to boot camp all the different types of personalities and intelligence levels in this world. Being brought up in an Italian neighborhood, where nearly everyone was almost on the same level, although some were smarter than others, I was never exposed to the extreme opposites. Everyone I had grown up with had at least had a grade school education, most had high school, and some had college. Everyone was literate. Some of these recruits could barely read; others had a tough time writing their names. I sort of felt sorry for them.

Private Wayne was one of those unfortunate individuals. On one occasion Sergeant Grant asked him to read something out of the Marine Corps guidebook. The private struggled horribly with just the first sentence.

"Private Wayne, you have to be one of the dumbest fuckers I have ever had the dishonor to have in my platoon. Don't they have schools where you come from, boy?"

"Sir, yes sir, they do."

"Well, if they have schools where you come from, boy, why the fuck are you so dumb?"

I really felt sorry for Wayne. It wasn't his fault he didn't go to school.

"Sir, my daddy died when I was a youngster and I had to go to work to help out at home, sir."

"Well, Wayne, at least you have a good reason for being stupid."

"Sir, yes sir."

The drilling was constant, along with numerous push-ups. I must say they were getting less frequent. Mostly everyone knew their right from the left by now.

When we were at attention in front of the mess hall, the sand fleas were working overtime. Those little critters bugged the hell out of us, with our constant companions pacing back and forth cussing us out. Each time we waited for our turn to enter the mess hall, it seemed like an eternity. I had never known anyone could discipline themselves, whether out of fear for their lives or otherwise, the way we did. It totally amazed me that the platoon could stand perfectly still for that length of time, without moving a muscle or eyelash, under the conditions we were in, with heat and fleas. A statue couldn't have had less motion.

In the mess hall, we were getting used to the servers and eating at attention.

For most of the days to this point, the screaming, calisthenics, and harassment continued at the same pace, never a moment's rest. One of the training methods for the DIs was to keep the recruits constantly occupied, so they never had time to collect their thoughts. Everything was geared to total submission to the Corps way of life, or you were out.

As time progressed, there was mumbling under certain recruits' breath "they weren't going to take too much more of this shit." It was apparent that some of the others just didn't have what it took to make it through boot camp. The weeding out process was well at work.

In the barracks, our details were very consistent. Everything had to be done by the Marine Corps manual. Each and every thing was spelled out in the manual. It instructed you how to make your rack, where everything went in your footlocker, how all of your clothes were folded, where everything was to be marked with your name, and so on.

Reveille was the same time every day, with the platoon falling out behind the barracks for our morning run. Almost everyone was getting in shape, but there were still a few that couldn't make the entire run. They weren't long for the Corps. After the run, it was time to get ready for chow. Each morning, after chow and a million calisthenics, the barracks was cleaned from top to bottom, including the head. A white-glove inspection of the entire area followed. If there was one piece of lint, one speck of dirt, or one water spot on the faucets, we paid dearly for it. Bunk drills were one of the favorites of Sergeant Grant. I swear he must have gotten his rocks off doing things the way he did. He was without a doubt an extremist and a real wacko.

After the barracks were cleaned, we fell outside for more drill practice and scores of push-ups. We drilled for hours upon end, and believe it or not, things began to shape up, not much at this point, but a far cry better than day one. By this time it was time for chow (lunch).

The system never changed. Breakfast, clean, and drill. Lunch, drill, and drill. Supper, drill, straighten the barracks, shower, then hit the racks. The calisthenics were never-ending. Every other night, when Sergeant Grant was on duty, I was reintroduced to the green wienie. I was used to getting the beating by now. But boot camp was getting to me. The nights Sergeant Bail was there, I did massive amounts of exercises with the makeshift barbell.

One night after chow when everyone was standing at attention in front of their bunks after supper, Sergeant Grant made the announcement that we could write home, if we had one. We were all issued writing paper and pens. He was pacing up and down the squad bay in his usual manner and running his mouth.

"It is my moral obligation as your drill instructor to let you shit birds write home to your mommies and daddies and let them know that you are not getting your asses kicked down here. I don't want you pussies' families writing or calling down here to see if you girls are still alive. I don't want anyone to think that their babies are getting kicked around here at Parris Island. Do you ladies read me?"

"Sir, yes sir."

There was sure a message in that statement.

"Are there any of you pussies that are getting your ass kicked down here?"

"Sir, no sir."

"The Marine Corps has issued some paper, pen, and envelopes for those of you dummies that can write. You will only be issued these articles one time. When you have used these articles up, you will buy more at your expense. You will have twenty minutes to write. The only persons you will write to are your mommies and daddies. There will not be any love letters written to your girlfriends, trying to impress on them how tough you are. When you are writing letters, or things of that nature, you will never sit on your bunks; you will sit on your footlockers. Is that clear?"

"Sir, yes sir."

A lot of thoughts were passing through my mind—if I dared to write home and tell them how we were being treated down here. Probably they wouldn't care or believe me. They would say this was part of the training. I didn't know if the DIs screened the mail. If they found out I had complained, I'd be dead. I never cried on my parents' shoulders before, so why start now? The best thing to do, I thought, was write a short, sweet letter saying I had gotten here all right and things were okay.

Taps sounded each night at the same time, ending another glorious day here at Paradise Island. The trumpet player must have been a reject from the Louie Armstrong band. He couldn't hit the right note with a sledgehammer. No one said the Corps was big on talent.

This meant for all the troops but one it was time to pass out again and forget their troubles for a few hours. For Private Iacampo, it meant the green wienie, getting hammered once more by Godzilla. Sergeant Grant had mastered the pronunciation of my last name by now and would scream it out as soon as the lights went out. I would charge down the hallway and report as directed. It all depended on what kind of mood he was in, as to how many times I had to beat the pine. By this time I was getting smarter. I began pounding the pine with the palm of my hand, instead of my knuckles. Live and learn. I wasn't looking forward to getting clobbered, but at least I knew what was coming. I would double over after getting hit and fall on the floor the same way each time. After every blasting session, he would chew my ass out and dismiss me to the squad bay.

Chapter 11

Characters

The personalities were varied among the recruits. There were people from all nationalities. Some recruits were clean, some dirty, some smart, some dumb, and some couldn't be described. There were one or two of them that bragged about having sex with their sisters. Maybe they ran out of sheep. Whether they were just bragging or not I didn't know. By the looks of some of them, I'd believe anything they told me. There were some guys who had never seen snow. Some didn't have indoor plumbing. Asking some of them to take a shower was like cutting off their arms. The only thing they ever used water for was to boil their moonshine.

A little at a time, some of the brood were getting weeded out. They couldn't take the regimentation, discipline, physical activity, or harassment. Not that it was easy for anyone, but some people have more backbone than others. That was what the Corps wanted, people with big balls that could take the heat. I had some compassion for the guys that really couldn't cut it, but there were one or two that were considered malingerers.

One such quitter was a kid from New Orleans named Parker. According to what everyone heard, this kid's old man was supposed to have some big bucks and some political influence. He was going to do his best to pull strings and get his kid out of boot camp. Parker must have gotten the word home to his parents about just what was happening here at

Paradise Island. If I could take the ass kicking I was taking and not complain, I couldn't have sympathy for anyone else who did complain. The whole thing boiled down to the fact that Parker couldn't cut it and was going to try to get out, any way he could. He began telling some of the other guys he wasn't going to take this shit from anyone; he was getting out. But daddy (that is what they call them down south; we called them "the old man") couldn't pay enough people off; they had to go to plan number two.

About two weeks into boot camp, little Parker started acting like a fag. As we all know, the Corps did not allow homosexuals in its ranks. He started walking and talking like a gay person. The wardens weren't fooled by his charade. They knew that he wasn't like that when he arrived at PI, but they had to play this pretense out. They started to harass the make-believe homosexual every way they knew, and they were pros. The good old boys pulled out every stop to try to catch the poor little rich kid, but the make-believe gay stood fast with his act and would not waver.

If the two wardens could prove that Parker was faking his role, he would be discharged with a BCD (bad conduct discharge). If he truly were gay, he would have been given a medical discharge. In the 1950s, when patriotism was at an all-time high in the USA, a BCD would be unacceptable to most employers or other people of authority. It was not the thing to have on one's record.

DIs had a distinct hatred for cowards and people with no backbone and did everything in their power to eliminate them from the Corps. Parker was a prime target. All of the goings-on with him were blessings in disguise. The more time the DIs took trying to trap this pretend homosexual, the less time they had to harass the rest of the platoon. Needless to say, we were not totally forgotten. But they did work on this guy for twenty-four hours a day. They woke him up in the middle of the night, constantly badgering him. One thing they had to do for their own protection was keep their hands off the bogus gay. As Parker's family was in on the game, he sure could have gotten word to them that he was getting beaten. So "hands off" was the policy. They tried to beat him to death with their mouths.

"So, you like sucking dicks, do you, boy? You know what the Marine Corps thinks of cocksuckers, don't you, boy? I heard fags like you like to take it in the ass. Is that right, boy? What do you like better, Parker, taking it in the ass or sucking dicks?" Sergeant Grant was so close to Parker with all of his ranting, he couldn't get any closer. While he was screaming, he was spraying Parker with saliva. All Sergeant Grant was waiting for was for Parker to make a slipup in one of his answers; then he would nail him.

All of the responses from the New Orleans kid were: "Yes, sir," and "No, sir." They had him do thousands of push-ups, sit-ups, and squat jumps, but he kept up the act. He scrubbed GI cans, cleaned the head and floors with a toothbrush, and had every shit detail conceivable. He wouldn't budge.

"You'd better never get close to me, boy. I can't stand lookin' at a cocksucker. If I had my way, boy, I'd take all you fags on a one-way trip through the swamps. We know you're not a fag boy, you're just a fuckin' quitter, and I don't know what's worse."

If Parker put as much effort into being a marine as he did into acting gay, he probably would have made a good marine. If anything could be said in his behalf, he had balls of steel. He took ten times the verbal punishment I ever did.

When the two sergeants exhausted all of the tricks in the book and saw they weren't getting anywhere with Parker, they were bound by military rules of conduct to have him see a doctor.

Parker was marched to the doctor's office like he was a prisoner, as he should have been. If he really was gay, he would have received more sympathy, but he got none from anyone. By this time, everyone in the platoon was against him.

I am sure that this was not the first time the doctor had to examine someone for this. If the person was really a homosexual, he had to be handled with kid gloves. Any abuse could mean big trouble for the USMC.

The regimental doctor had to use the same techniques in his exam as if Parker really was gay, but he had been told by the DIs that they suspected Parker was faking. All of the normal interviewing procedures were not getting the doctor anywhere. As a last resort, he stood in front of the make-believe homosexual and pulled down his zipper, saying, "If you're really a fag, then take care of business." When that happened, Parker dropped to his knees to complete the charade. If he had to go out that way, so be it. The doctor quickly stepped back and ordered Parker out of his office, where Sergeant Grant was waiting.

Parker returned to the barracks the same way he had been taken to the doctor's office, like a prisoner. None of the other recruits would even look at him, let alone talk to him. He had accomplished his mission, but I don't know if the price for being a coward was worth it. After about two or three days, we never saw him again.

Sergeants Grant and Bail by now knew almost everyone by their name. There were no first names in Marine Corps boot camp; you were always addressed by your last name. Privates Wayne and Green were no strangers to the two wardens.

Wayne was a white kid from down south somewhere, and Green was his black clone. Both were uneducated people, both from some hillbilly town. Both were about six-six. Due to their size, they were always visible, and fair prey for Sergeant Grant.

"Privates Wayne and Green, you're both so tall and so

dumb, you're probably brothers and don't know it. Are you two brothers and aren't telling anyone?" All they could do was take the abuse and answer, "Yes, sir," or, "No, sir."

In boot camp no matter how hard the DI came down on you, you'd better always agree with him, if you knew what was good for you. This was a form of entertainment for them, and you'd better not spoil their fun. These DIs were not normal people; they had a distorted sense of humor. At PI, when you were right you were wrong, and when you were wrong, you were really in trouble. It was a no-win situation.

"Private Wayne, would you like to sleep with my sister?" Sergeant Grant asked.

"Sir, no sir."

"Did you say 'no sir,' boy? You mean my sister isn't good enough for you, boy?"

Very confused, Wayne responded, "Sir, yes sir."

"What do you mean, Wayne, you want to fuck my sister? I should kick your dumb ass all over this island. You'd better never say you want to fuck my sister again, boy. Do you read me?"

"Sir, yes sir."

By that time, Wayne was a complete wreck.

Wayne's and Green's feet were so big, they had to wear tennis shoes through the better part of boot camp. They had to have tailor-made shoes.

They were a real combination. "Your fuckin' brains ought to be as big as your feet. You two wouldn't be too bad off," Sergeant Grant told them.

Private Smythe was another kid from a southern state. He was so afraid of Sergeant Grant that when the sergeant merely talked to him he would shake in his boots. When Sergeant Grant yelled at him, his knees would knock. When DIs singled out someone that they could get to, they really put the coals to him. Smythe was their man.

One day, Sergeant Grant got right into Smythe's face and started to work on him. His knees were knocking so loudly, I could hear them from the other end of the squad bay. He was nose to nose and toes to toes with the sergeant. That was Sergeant Grant's favorite position for communicating. "Boy, do you like me, boy?"

Smythe knew whatever answer he gave would be the wrong one, so he took a chance and answered, "Sir, yes sir, I do like you."

Still in Smythe's face, Sergeant Grant answered, "Let me tell you something, Private Smythe. Likin' is lovin', and lovin' is fuckin', and you ain't fuckin' me, boy."

I thought Smythe was going to have a stroke right on the spot. He lost any composure he had and began to cry.

"Get down and give me fifty push-ups, Smythe. I can't stand to see a pussy cry." That made Sergeant Grant's day.

When a person arrives at PI and he is skinny, he usually gains weight and puts on muscle. If he is fat, he usually loses the excess weight and trims down. The exceptions to the rule are the people who can't lose the excess weight by the conventional method of training. These poor souls are sent to a special platoon where weight loss is their main undertaking. This platoon is appropriately called the Fat Man's Platoon. In life, there are pluses and minuses to most everything. The plus to the Fat Man's Platoon was that you eventually dropped your excess weight. The minus was after you dropped the excess weight, you started boot camp all over again. It was conceivable that someone could spend six months in basic training, between the Fat Man's Platoon and the regular training—a fate worse than death.

The Italian kid that I met on the train coming to PI and that shared the bunk with me was one of the unfortunates to have to go through the Fat Man's Platoon. His name was Mancini. He was a very nice kid that came from Pennsylvania.

Coming from a traditional Italian family, he ate more than he should, and he had a problem shedding the weight. At first he made a valid attempt to lose the excess baggage, but to no avail, and he was shipped out to join the rest of the fat people. Shortly before Platoon 2028 was ready to graduate, I saw him doing his laundry next to our barracks. He looked terrific but was depressed, since he had to start basic training all over. In total he spent about twenty-four weeks in hell. I really felt sorry for him.

Chapter 12
Still in Our Faces

The harassment and regimentation continued at a very strong pace, trying to eliminate the weak at heart. Through it all, we could see a reduction in the harassment. It still existed, but not at the frantic pace it had been when we started. All of the recruits were still deadly afraid of Sergeant Grant. Sergeant Bail was like a giant sand flea. He was always buzzing but never bit anyone. By now we were getting used to their ways. I compared it to my old man kicking my ass. It had really bothered me, but the more he did it, the less effect it had on me. As long as the platoon towed the line, did what we were supposed to, and took a slap once in a while, Sergeant Grant was happy. The green wienie never stopped. Sergeant Grant took out all hostilities on me.

With about two or three weeks under our belts, we caught a little break in the action. There was a test that all recruits had to take, called an MOS (military occupational status) test. It was a written test that gave the Marine Corps insight into what field the recruit was best suited for when boot camp was completed. All MOSs had their own identification number.

There was a separate building used especially for the MOS testing. The platoon was half-herded and half-marched there. By now mostly everyone knew their left from their right. There had been a measurable improvement in our drilling skills. The test lasted about two hours. The people with normal educations finished in about forty-five minutes; the others took quite a bit longer. This was really the first time since our newly appointed guardians had picked us up from the receiving barracks that we could rest our brains for more than five minutes. It reminded me of when I was back in school, sitting at the desk taking the exam. There was no yelling and carrying on from the DIs. They were outside having a smoke, another thing we didn't have the luxury of doing. When everyone was finished with the test, we were back to reality again.

"Come, ladies, let's get into formation. The party is over; get your dead asses squared away. Jesus H. Christ. I can't believe you girls remembered what place you were in in formation. Will wonders never cease. Maybe there is some hope for you bunch of shit birds yet. Attention. Left face, forward march, double-time march. Left, right, left, right, left."

We ran halfway around the base and ended up behind the barracks, where we worked on some of our drills and calisthenics.

"You ladies had a pretty easy morning, and I don't want you to get spoiled. There are no such things as easy days here on my island. Isn't that right, girls?"

"Sir, yes sir."

"Now to make up for the vacation you had this morning, we are going to get the kinks out of your asses with some jumping jacks. They will be done in the following manner. You will place your hands behind your head and lock your fingers together. To my count, you will squat up and down like a frog, and, ladies, keep it together. You will keep your backs straight, shoulders back, and look straight ahead. If you do not keep in time, you will do this all day."

"Sir, yes sir."

"Ready, one-two-three-four-five-six-seven. Keep it together, girls; we can do these all day. What's the matter with you shit birds? Can't you stay with the count? One-two-three-four-five-six, come on, girls, keep it together."

This time was one of the first times we did squat jumps, and everyone was falling all over the place.

"Get down for push-ups, girls; let's see if you can get these right. One-two-three-four-five-six-seven-eight."

By the time Sergeant Grant was finished with us, we must have done four hundred squat jumps and that many push-ups. I would rather do push-ups any day; the squat jumps were murder on the calves and knees.

The rest of that day went by with the usual confusion. Lunch and supper came quickly. We never had five minutes to ourselves and lost track of time. In between the meals we did more calisthenics and more drills. After supper it was time for barracks cleaning.

Showers were taken according to where your rack was located in the squad bay. A lot of bumping and shoving always took place going in and out of the head. Mostly all of it was ignored, due to the circumstances. That night as I headed into the shower, I turned the corner sharply and ran right into big, bad Jackson. He was about an inch taller than I was, and when I collided with him, my head hit him in the mouth.

"Watch where you're going, motherfucker," he blurted out.

"Keep your big ass out of my way," I replied.

A little shoving and pushing ensued, but no one noticed. A few dirty looks followed the shoving match, and we both went on our ways. I think we were both smart enough not to start a fight, with Sergeant Bail around the corner, but a confrontation was inevitable.

With everyone showered, we were all standing in front of our racks at attention. This was the first night Sergeant Grant was not on duty. Sergeant Bail announced that all the rules that applied when Sergeant Grant was on duty applied now.

Sergeant Bail was walking up and down the squad bay, acting as tough as he could. Thank God he was of a milder nature. No one could have survived two Sergeant Grants.

"When you ladies hit the rack, there will be no talking, no getting out of the rack. I want complete silence. Private Iacampo, report to me on the double."

"Sir, yes sir."

I ran down the hall to his quarters. I had some idea what to expect; phase two of the green wienie was about to go into action. I punched the pine as hard as I could with the palm of my hand, hoping that one time would be enough for Sergeant Bail. He didn't make me try to pulverize my hand the way his boss did.

"Sir, Private Iacampo is reporting as ordered, sir."

"Front and center, boy," Sergeant Bail replied.

I took one step forward, did a left face, and concentrated my gaze at the eyeballs pasted on the window, as I did with Sergeant Grant.

"Private Iacampo," Sergeant Bail said, talking out of the side of his mouth, trying as hard as he could to be as tough as his boss, "you have fucked up big time at the processing center, and Sergeant Grant has instructed me to have you do PT for one half hour each night I am on duty."

As hard as he tried, he couldn't play the tough guy role very well. He reminded me of Mickey Rooney trying to play a John Wayne role. In the hallway opposite his quarters I did curls, military presses, with the makeshift barbell. The muscles in my arms and shoulders were so tight from all the exercises I had been doing, I thought my arms were going to fall off. He didn't watch me for the entire time. He would watch for five minutes and go back into his quarters for a few minutes. It didn't appear to me that his heart and soul were totally into what he was doing as a DI. In his absence, I did a lot of grunting and groaning to make it sound like I was busting my butt. All in all, I would do about twenty out of the thirty minutes of exercise I was supposed to do. I wasn't sure after I finished the PT, if I was better off getting one good shot to the gut and getting it over with, rather than losing a half hour's sleep doing exercise I didn't need.

Chapter 13
The Pride of the Corps (DIs)

Most of the DIs came from the southern states, and some of them were still fighting the Civil War. Still, after all these years, they couldn't accept the fact that the northern boys had kicked their asses. Needless to say, the hard-core DIs were doubly hard on the northern troops. While under the cover of the Smokey the Bear hats at Parris Island, they had their opportunity to try to get even with the conquerors. It wasn't bad enough being from a northern state, but if you were from Cleveland, New York, New Jersey, Detroit, or Chicago, you really had problems. If that wasn't enough, if you happened to be from any of the above and your last name ended in a vowel, as it often did in the Italian nationality, as Sergeant Grant said, you'd better give your soul to God, cause your ass was his. Good Italian people have always had a cross to bear because of the bum racketeers.

One day in the barracks, after morning chow, Sergeant Grant must have had a bad hangover and he was going to take his anger out on me. Nose to nose and toes to toes, he started on me. I could smell the liquor on his breath when he was twenty feet away from me.

"So, Private Iacampo, I see you are from Cleveland, are you, boy?'

"Sir, yes sir."

"You're one of those guys who thinks you're a badass and carry a switchblade in your pocket, aren't you, boy?"

"Sir, no sir."

"We like tough guys like you down here, Private Iacampo. You already proved you don't know when to keep your fuckin' mouth shut. Isn't that right, Private Iacampo?

"I think you are one of those dago pussies, aren't you, boy? We don't think highly of you so-called badasses down here. Are you a badass, Iacampo?"

"Sir, no sir."

If nothing else, I was learning in boot camp when to keep my remarks to myself. If I had told Sergeant Grant exactly what I thought of him at that time, someone would have been fishing me out of the swamp. As long as you answered the DIs' questions the way they wanted you to, you were all right. But no matter how you answered, sometimes yes was wrong and so was no. Flip a coin and take a chance.

The majority of the DIs I saw were guys in their late twenties or early thirties. Ninety-nine percent of them were in extremely good physical condition. They ran wherever their platoon ran, and most of the time backward, so they could watch the herd. I would have to say that the cream of the crop, physically speaking, were picked to be DIs. It was difficult for me to understand, at the time, that these DIs had to display the type of aggressiveness they did to get results from their troops. Some, like Sergeant Grant went way overboard, but in retrospect, I think I'd rather be trained by him than by someone too soft.

The words *squared away* were coined for the DIs. Spit and polish was an obsession for most of them. Most of them looked like they just walked out of the *Marine Corps Gazette*. The brass on their uniforms was shined to a high luster, their boots and shoes sparkled, and a person could cut his finger on the creases in their clothing. They were what the Corps was all about.

There was a staff sergeant named Hancock in the barracks next to us. I never had any close contact with him, but after things cooled off we were able to talk to the other recruits that lived next door. We shared the same outdoor wash rack, where our laundry was done by hand, with Fells naphtha soap and a scrub brush. Sergeant Hancock was definitely a fanatic, but only of a different nature. He stood about six-one, with reddish brown hair and a rosy complexion from hitting the bottle. He was so obsessed with his appearance, he would actually walk ten miles or better so as not to ride in a Jeep and get creases in his pants. After doing anything, he would wash his hands and clean his fingernails. There were stories spread about him that at night when he went home (he was married and lived off base) his wife and daughter would have to greet him at the front door at attention, and then he inspected his house for any dirt or lint. It had to be impossible, living with a nut like him. One of the next-door recruits told me that one day they really knew he had flipped. They saw him wiping the dust out of the twist in the top of a metal hanger with a damp cloth. Between the booze and the Corps, his mind was really fried.

Staff Sergeant Bragg was assigned to Platoon 2028 about halfway through our training. It was his first and last assignment as a DI. He had the unfortunate problem of treating the recruits as human beings. That did not fit into the Corps program. He had to be a very good marine to make it to staff sergeant, as the Corps did not hand out promotions easily. His biggest problem, as far as the Corps was concerned, was that he wasn't a sadist. He probably could have made it as a junior DI, but not as a senior DI. But as he was a staff sergeant, he was being groomed for the top job. He spent a few weeks with us and disappeared. It was obvious Sergeant Grant and Sergeant Bragg didn't see eye to eye. Sergeant Bail, from what we could tell, got along very well with him, But Sergeant Grant was the undisputed *boss*.

Staff Sergeant Grant was a person with an indescribable personality. I don't even like to use the word *personality,* as he had none. I could never figure out if he was naturally hostile or if the Corps had made him that way. He had a manner that sent chills up and down the spines of all his recruits. No one could have been born the way he was. Something or someone had to push this guy over the edge. On top of being downright nasty, he was a crude bastard. He smoked like a chimney and drank like a fish. Although he was in moderately good physical condition, it was obvious the booze was taking its toll on him. Every day he looked a little worse than the day before, if that was possible. He must have written the harassment and de-moralizing guidebook for the Corps. There wasn't a cussword he didn't know, and he used all of them with a great deal of frequency. From the day I was assigned to Platoon 2028, the man, using the word loosely, never said a word to me or anyone else in the platoon that wasn't in the way of an ass chewing. He was the downright meanest person I had ever met, and he made a lasting impression on me—not a good impression, but a lasting one. Most days when he reported for duty, you could smell him coming before you saw him, due to all the booze on his breath. When he had put on a real bender the night before, the PT and harassment were intensified. Platoon 2028 had to pay for his sins.

Drinking in the Marine Corps was an enormous problem. Drinking and the Corps went hand in hand. If a marine didn't drink, he was an outcast. In the Marine Corps charter, there was an unwritten law that three things were necessary to qualify as a good marine: having the ability to fight, drink like a fish, and be a womanizer—but not necessarily in that order.

Sergeant Bail was of medium height, slender but well built. He always kept himself in good physical condition. He was one of the marines that lived by the book, but not a fanatic. He probably took a nip once in a while, but only in moderation. He couldn't hold a candle to his boss in the harassement department. He tried to be mean and nasty like Sergeant Grant but didn't have it in him. He made a very good junior drill instructor and carried out all of Sergeant Grant's orders. Of the two of them, Sergeant Bail was the more polished. He had teaching ability—that was necessary to be a good DI—and also had the knowledge and patience to instruct us on the finer points of being a marine.

Shakedowns (seeking involuntary donations) were not uncommon among some of the low-class DIs. It was just before Christmas in 1958 when our senior DI made his move on the platoon. For the first time since we had met our master, his tone of voice was not as belligerent as usual. As dumb as we recruits had been told we were, we smelled a rat. This guy was acting totally out of character. Sergeant Bail knew nothing about this scam; he was not on duty that night.

Sergeant Grant had all the platoon gather in the middle of the squad bay, as he had done many times before for different lectures.

"Okay, ladies, as you well know, Christmas is right around the corner, and I have a slight problem. After a close check of my finances, I see that I can't get my wife and kids everything they want for Christmas. If I come home empty-handed, they will be very pissed off at me. If my wife and kids are pissed off at me, that means I will be pissed off at you. I will make things here unbearable. [I don't know what he thought conditions were like already.] If we want to eliminate that possibility, I am gonna leave this pail in the middle of the squad bay and go to my quarters. If I return and there is a good amount in it, your Christmas and mine will be much happier." And that was Sergeant Grant's scam.

In boot camp we were paid once a month and had only a few dollars on hand at any time for necessary items. I think at that time we were paid $78 per month. Only a small portion was given to us while training, the remainder when we graduated. Everyone in the platoon put one or two dollars in the pail in order to try to ease our suffering. We didn't know if he spent the money on booze or if he really needed it for his family. But, from our point of view, it was money well spent. That was the first and last time we were ever shaken down.

The Marine Corps had no room in its ranks for the weak at heart. It was the sole responsibility of the DIs to keep up the high traditions of the Corps and to eliminate the people that couldn't cut the training. The Corps always had the reputation of being the toughest branch of the armed services, and they intended to keep it that way.

It was never clear to me whether Sergeant Grant hated me because of the bad start I had with him or if he wanted to see just what I was made of. He gave me his best shots, both in the gut and psychologically, and I took it in stride. He didn't know I had grown up getting my ass kicked, so his act wasn't new to me, although it was more severe than I had ever experienced. He used every technique that he knew to break me and my spirit. I must say at times I bent, but I never broke. He got into my face on a regular basis and cussed me out like a dog. I did calisthenics by the thousands. Every time the platoon did something new, Private Iacampo was the first one in line. Sergeant Grant gave me every shit detail he could think of. I was sticking it out as a matter of pride. If I gave in to this sadist, I would go home defeated, and that I wouldn't do. It wasn't legal for a DI to whack a recruit like he was hitting me. This type of behavior was something that everyone knew about but ignored until someone finked or someone got hurt. He may have thought that someday I would get pissed off enough to take a swing at him—then he could get me without repercussions—but I wasn't that dumb. In my own way I was trying to find a positive side to all of this. I was developing the strongest set of stomach muscles and the toughest constitution at PI. By the time I graduated I gained thirty-six pounds, and none of it was fat.

Chapter 14

Slack Was Coming

One of the novel things we did as a platoon was sort of a morale booster. (We needed all the help we could get.) While running in formation, we would sing songs that the DIs in all their wisdom had made up. Here are some examples:

> Got all shot up in the Russian war, honey, honey.
> Got all shot up in the Russian war, babe, babe.
> All shot up in the Russian war.
> They buried me with a Russian whore.
> Honey, oh, baby mine.
> Go to your left, your right, your left.

[And it would be repeated over and over.]

> If the army and the navy
> Ever looked on heaven's scenes
> They would find their wives are shacking up
> With United States marines.

[And repeat.]

> Gonna get a three-day pass, honey, honey.
> Gonna get a three-day pass, babe, babe.
> Gonna get a three-day pass,
> Then I'm gonna get a piece of ass.
> Honey, oh, baby mine.

[And repeat.]

After a while, things began to settle down a little. By then, Platoon 2028 had about one month under its belt, and the conditions began to lighten up. For the most part, we were getting acclimated to the Marine Corps way of life. It was a very big adjustment on each and everyone's part. No normal human being could have been prepared for what PI and Sergeant Grant had in store for us. The screaming, yelling, and harassment were ever-present, but slowly diminishing now. Maybe the good old boys were running out of gas, but I doubt it.

Each morning we were awakened to the music of one of the good sergeants beating on the racks with an iron pipe. We would fall out behind the barracks and begin with PT, then our morning runs. The distance of the runs consistently became longer, as all the troops were finally getting into shape. It wasn't long before we were running five to eight miles at a crack without a problem. Platoon 2028 began to look like marines. Even the odd couple, Wayne and Green, started to resemble marines. Back at the barracks, we would be dismissed to get ready for morning chow. The stampedes in and out of the barracks no longer existed. In front of the mess hall, while we awaited our turn to enter, we were able to stand at ease. It was amusing to watch new recruits march alongside us and be put through the same torture we had been put through. I felt sorry for them, but this was called paying your dues. In the mess hall, the food was no longer slung at us; we were served in a normal fashion. We no longer had to eat at attention; that sure helped with the laundry. After chow, we could fall out outside the mess hall and stand at ease until everyone was back in formation. We were marched back to the barracks, instead of being herded. We almost felt human again.

Our living quarters were cleaned each and every day,

from top to bottom. There wasn't one square inch of the head or the squad bay that didn't get washed and polished. Everything was scrubbed, buffed, scraped, waxed, washed, and then inspected. Depending on the mood of Sergeant Grant, which was usually nasty because of his hangovers, we usually did the cleaning process twice, after about twenty minutes of push-ups and squat jumps.

Lunch- and suppertime came and went, with a good amount of marching and drilling in between. Believe it or not, it was almost becoming enjoyable, marching and drilling with hardly anyone screwing up. From time to time the platoon's black and white clones (Wayne and Green) would forget their right from left, and push-ups would soon follow. They were starting to catch a slap from the few members of the platoon from time to time, to help them stay in line.

On several occasions, Jackson and I had a few words or exchanged a dirty look or two. Our dislike for each other became even greater. I was sort of looking forward to the day he and I locked horns, as I needed to vent my frustration on someone. It wouldn't be long.

Small groups began to form in the platoon. The hillbillies, the blacks, and the ethnics started to form their little cliques. I was informally elected to represent city boys and the Italian group. The hillbillies had a kid named Wilmar as their leader, and Jackson was the kingpin for the blacks.

It began to remind me of being back home, with the different cliques. There was never any hostility between us, and everyone got along fairly well.

Chapter 15

The Smoking Lamp

Roughly four to five weeks had passed since we began our training, and the smokers in the platoon had not had a cigarette. I never really thought about smoking except when I saw one of the DIs puffing on a cigarette.

One day as we were standing at ease, in front of the barracks, waiting to be dismissed, Sergeant Grant made an announcement. If the platoon behaved itself and deserved it, the smoking lamp would be lit after every meal. The smoking lamp was figurative. If it was lit, smoking was permitted; if not, no smoking. Having a cigarette on PI was a reward, not a given thing. It was all up to Godzilla.

Traditionally, the smallest member of the platoon was dubbed the "house mouse" by the DI. His duty was to be the runner for the DIs. Whenever they needed something, the house mouse would run and get it for them. Platoon 2028's house mouse was a cute little guy named Morris that everyone liked.

"Private Morris," Sergeant Grant called out, "in my quarters, on my desk, is a box with cigarettes in it! You will run up on the double and fetch the box!" (The house mouse was the only one ever allowed in the DI's quarters by himself.)

"Sir, yes sir," Morris responded.

About 80 percent of the platoon smoked, and they were shocked by the announcement. I had not had a cigarette since my train ride to the island. When Private Morris returned with the box, Sergeant Grant instructed him to pass out a cigarette to whoever wanted one.

"Listen up, ladies. It is a privilege to be given a cigarette in my platoon, and the privilege can be taken away faster than it was given. If any one of you in the platoon fucks up—I don't care if you are a smoker or not—the smoking lamp will be put out. I don't give a fuck what brand of cigarette you smoke; you will take what the house mouse gives you. The smoking lamp is only lit when I say it's lit. Do you ladies read me?"

"Sir, yes sir."

I almost passed out when I inhaled my first drag. It felt like the first cigarette I had ever smoked. Just about everyone that was smoking was hacking his brains out. All of our lungs had been smoke-free for about five weeks. This was the first real bonus we had had since our pilgrimage began, and it didn't agree with us.

"If I catch anyone abusing this privilege, I will cut the smoking out altogether. Do you read me?"

"Sir, yes sir."

The platoon finally had something to look forward to. Those that didn't smoke enjoyed the free time they were getting.

A new term was about to be introduced to us: *field stripping*.

"When you ladies are finished with your cigarettes, you will split them along the seam of the cigarette. You will then separate the tobacco from the paper, throw it on the ground, and rub it in. This will prevent cigarette butts from accumulating all over my island. Is that clear?"

As time went on, we were allowed smoking privileges more often, but always under the watchful eyes of the DIs, and not without their permission. Smoking was never permitted in the barracks.

Through their routine inspection of the area, the DIs

began to find cigarette butts under the barracks. All the barracks were set up off the ground for ventilation. Without saying anything to anyone, they began to watch for the culprit.

Private Norris was a red-headed creep with freckles all over his face. I didn't like him from the time I saw him. It wasn't only me; most of the other recruits also had a dislike for the kid. He must have been addicted to smoking. Anyone that would take a chance and sneak out of the barracks after taps to have a smoke had to be either addicted, stupid, or, in Norris's case, both.

About an hour after taps sounded one night, we heard a commotion in the barracks. It was Sergeant Grant, dragging the redheaded offender by one of his big ears into the squad bay. (His ears stuck out about two inches.)

With everyone still half-asleep, Sergeant Grant was screaming at the top of his lungs. "Everyone get out of your racks and stand at attention! In the past few days I have noticed cigarette butts under and next to the barracks! Through some investigation, I have found this sneak, Private Norris, going out of the barracks after taps and smoking! Not only did Private Norris violate the smoke lamp rules, but I have lost a considerable amount of sleep trying to catch him! When I don't get my sleep, it really pisses me off! Norris not only fucked himself up by this stupid act, but now the entire platoon has lost the smoking privileges! There will be no smoking until further notice!"

Norris was shaking in his boots. He knew not only was he going to pay for his sins with Sergeant Grant, but he had platoon justice to deal with also.

"After Private Norris eats a pack of his favorite brand, he is going to drink a gallon of hot water to wash them down. Then he will smoke a pack while under a GI can. If you ladies ever want to smoke again, I would recommend that you teach your fellow platoon member a good lesson." All the while

Norris was standing next to Sergeant Grant during the chastising he was getting little slaps in the back of his head.

It was almost worth losing our smoking rights to see Norris being put through the wringer. Unfortunately for him, he smoked Pall Malls, the longest cigarette on the market, so there was all the more to eat. After he half-choked to death from his main course, he washed it down with some of PI's finest hot water. Though Norris was nearly puking from that, two of the recruits held a GI can over his head while he smoked one cigarette after another until he smoked a whole pack. This boy was really sick. He looked like he had been on an ocean liner for a month and was seasick. To complete Norris's punishment, Sergeant Grant went into his quarters while the platoon did a job on Norris. We didn't leave any scars on him, just some sore ribs and a black eye. He never did sneak out for a smoke again.

Chapter 16
A Marine's Only Friend

In the eyes of the Corps, there is only one thing that a marine can depend on beside his platoon in the time of battle, his rifle. It is the most sacred possession a marine can have. He is issued a rifle in boot camp, and this weapon stays with him for most of his entire enlistment. The biggest mistake anyone can make is to call his rifle a gun. You might as well call the DI's mother a hooker.

The day our rifles were issued at the armory, we double-timed it back to the barracks with the rifles at port arms (diagonal across our chest), great exercise for the arms. Once in the barracks, one at a time, we stood in the middle of the squad bay, on top of a GI can, with the rifles in our right hands and our genitals in the left and recited the Marine Corps creed for the rifle: "THIS IS MY RIFLE, AND THIS MY GUN, THIS ONE FOR FIGHTING, AND THIS ONE IS FOR FUN." After we repeated that verse several times, the lecture began.

"You shit birds have just been issued the M-1 rifle. It is a clip-fed semiautomatic weapon. This is the only thing that will save your life in the time of battle. It is your only friend. You will, and I repeat will, never call this weapon a gun; it is a rifle. Your gun is between your legs, if some of you have one. You will always keep this weapon clean. You will take better care of this weapon than you would your girlfriends' tits. You maggots will learn this weapon inside out. If you do not take care of this weapon, this weapon will not take care of you. When your weapons are not being cleaned or in use, they will be stacked in the rifle racks in the middle of the squad bay. You will know which is your rifle at all times. Do I make myself clear?"

"Sir, yes sir."

"Tonight you shitheads are gonna sleep with your rifles. You will sleep with your rifle on your right side, and you will not lay on your rifle. If I catch anyone sleeping on his rifle, he will put his dick in the bolt and slam it. This is your only friend in the Corps. You will respect it, and it will take care of you."

"Sir, yes sir."

Hour by hour we spent getting acquainted with our only friend. Aside from our drilling and our personal hygiene, our rifles received more attention than anything. The cleaning and oiling of the weapons became a daily chore. The stock and grip were treated by rubbing linseed oil into their wooden surface. With the proper application, they would shine like a pair of shoes. The chamber was cleaned with oil and a toothbrush. The bore was cleaned with a metal bore brush, lightly oiled, and swabbed out with a cloth patch.

There are always people in this world that are constantly cutting corners. One of these people was my good friend Private Wilmar. He tried a shortcut with everything he did, which usually backfired on him. He thought if he left a rifle patch in the bore of his rifle, it would keep the dirt and lint out. Instead, unbeknownst to him, leaving the cloth patch in the barrel of the rifle made it sweat and rust. During one of the frequent inspections, he forgot to take the patch out and got caught, again, by none other than Sergeant Grant.

"Private Wilmar, you have to be one of the dumbest fuckin' recruits I have ever run across. Don't you know, Private Wilmar, that if you have a patch in your weapon and you fire the weapon, it will blow up in your goddamn face? You never leave a patch in your weapon, Private Wilmar. You think that you are smarter than me, Wilmar, but you always get caught.

Don't you, Wilmar?" He was getting the nose-to-nose routine from the boss.

"Sir, yes sir."

"Private Wilmar, I am gonna make sure that you never leave a patch in your weapon again. You will run around this parade ground with your rifle at port arms and repeat the following: 'I am a dumb motherfucker, and I will never leave a patch in my rifle again.' You will repeat that as long as you run, and as loud as you can. Is that clear, Wilmar?"

"Sir, yes sir."

I don't know if Sergeant Grant deliberately forgot about Wilmar or not, but he ran around the parade field for almost five hours, including missing chow.

Sergeant Grant had to be the mastermind of misery. The newest in his repertoire of harassment were jumping jacks in the shower fully clothed, with rifles and packs.

One day, for some reason, Platoon 2028 didn't have their act together, and Sergeant Grant was in a bad mood to start. "You ladies have really pissed me off today. You have two minutes to get fully clothed with your field jackets, helmets, packs, and rifles. When that is completed, you will get your dead asses in the shower."

When everyone was crammed into the shower room (God only knows how we got in there), we were instructed to turn on the water. While the water was running, Sergeant Grant made us do jumping jacks by the numbers.

"You ladies like to fuck around, do you? One-two-three-four-five-six-seven-eight."

We did jumping up and down for ten minutes. When the shower drill was over, beside our being soaked from head to toe, our best friends were drenched, and just about everyone had busted lips and black eyes from getting pushed around. It was the nastiest shot he had pulled yet. But never think the party is over until the party is over. He still had total control of the situation.

"You shit birds have ten minutes to clean up and get in front of your racks for inspection; that includes the head. We'll see if you fuck off anymore."

It was impossible to get the mess cleaned up in ten minutes. As we were not ready for inspection, a barrage of push-ups followed.

Learning to handle the rifle and all of the different maneuvers was an experience in itself. For the same reason it was difficult for some of the lamebrains to learn to march, it was more difficult for them to learn to handle the rifle and its maneuvers. As usual, every time someone messed up, the push-ups followed. Wayne and Green were still our main anchors.

"I don't know what the fuck to do with you two shitheads. It took you four weeks to learn your left from your right; now it's gonna take another month to teach you how to handle your weapons. I could teach a fuckin' monkey faster than you learn. I wish your mothers would have never had you two; they would have saved me a lot of aggravation."

Parade rest, port arms, left shoulder arms, right shoulder arms were some of the maneuvers we had to learn. All of these maneuvers had to be done simultaneously and with precision by the entire platoon. We spent hour after hour on the parade field practicing. God forbid if someone dropped his rifle. One day during drills, Private Amato dropped his best friend. He was a quiet, unassuming kid that never got into any trouble, until now. If he didn't talk once in a while, you didn't even know he was around. In Sergeant Grant's eyes, Amato would have been better off if he had gone AWOL.

"Jesus H. Christ, Private Amato, what the fuck would you do in the time of battle if you dropped your rifle?"

"Sir, I don't know, sir."

96

"Well, Private Amato, if you don't know, who the fuck does? If you fuck this weapon up during combat, the only thing you'll have left in your hand is your dick. How in the fuck are you going to shoot anyone with your dick?" It was another nose-to-nose ass chewing. I always marveled that Sergeant Grant didn't have a stroke during one of these episodes. "You will run around this parade field, with your rifle at port arms, until I tell you to stop. Is that clear, Amato?"

"Sir, yes sir."

It must have been at least two hours before Sergeant Grant let Amato stop and join the rest of the platoon.

After we mastered the maneuvers with the rifle, drilling became a pleasure. Platoon 2028 was staring to resemble a real Marine Corps platoon, rifles and all. Our confidence level was on the rise, and the harassment became less frequent. We started to feel like marines.

Chapter 17
Breaking the Monotony

From the beginning of boot camp, there were few things we were allowed to do, if any, that didn't pertain to our training. One of the only things that the Corps was obligated to let the recruits do was go to Sunday services. It was funny that so many people all of a sudden became religious. The biggest heathens were making the trip to Sunday mass. It was the only time in the week, since we began basic training, that we got to rest our brains and get a little slack from the DIs.

There were two different places that services were held. When the weather was inclement, services were held in the base chapel. When the weather was nice, services were held in the outside theater, which happened to be directly behind our barracks. The theater was like a drive-in theater with benches. Movies were shown there for the senior recruits about two months into their training, depending on their DI's discretion.

At the theater there were two long rows of benches, with about forty benches in each row. The first time the platoon went to services, we were seated on the left side. While we were seated, a platoon of women marines was marched in to the right of us.

The nickname for women marines was BAMs (Broad-Assed marines), something they didn't much care for. Each platoon of BAMs had a male DI and a female DI. Usually the female DI looked and acted like a prison warden, very unattractive and masculine. All of them were notorious for their foul mouths, like their male counterparts. There were always rumors floating around that the male DIs were having sex with some of the female recruits. I'm sure it did happen, but to what extent I don't know.

While we were seated, the BAMs were ushered to their seats. Before they were given the command to sit, their female warden said, "Eyes left. Take a good look over there, ladies; there is a mile of swinging dick there, and you ain't getting an inch of it." The next thing she said was: "When I say 'ready seats,' I want to hear seventy-five pussies hit that bench at one time. Ready seats." She made the girls get up and down about five times until there was one thud when their butts hit the benches.

I caught a glimpse of the girl I had met on the train coming to PI. I saw her a couple of other times in church but never had a chance to talk to her, just smile. I often wondered if she regretted joining the Corps to be with her boyfriend. By the looks of her, she didn't seem to be thrilled.

Chapter 18
I Still Didn't Learn

It was a couple of days before Christmas. The ever-so-gracious host at PI, Sergeant Grant, asked the platoon one night if anyone had any complaints or dislikes so far. What a loaded question.

"Private Iacampo, why the fuck can't you keep your big fuckin' mouth shut? What is it you don't like?"

At that point I should have been smart enough to keep my thoughts to myself, but I wasn't. I always felt that my opinion was necessary. *Wrong.*

"Sir," I began to register my complaint, "I have not been getting enough to eat in the chow hall."

"You haven't, Iacampo. Well, that is too fuckin' bad. But I'll tell you what, Private Iacampo. I'll see what I can do. We definitely want to make your stay at Parris Island a happy one." That didn't sound too convincing to me.

Suppertime on Christmas Day, Sergeant Grant was waiting for me at the beginning of the chow line. "So you're not getting enough to eat, are you, Iacampo. Follow me." As we went through the line, he had the guys on mess duty pile food on my tray six inches high. I had three turkey legs, three wings, white meat, a pound of mashed potatoes, dressing, and everything that went with the meal. The food was actually falling off the tray. "Iacampo, you will report to me with a clean tray, in ten minutes. Don't you give any food away. Is that clear? I want to make sure you have enough to eat so you aren't hungry anymore."

I went to the table I was assigned to and began stuffing food down my throat. I was eating so fast, I wasn't chewing half of the food. Luckily, a few of my friends were sitting at the table, and I sneaked some of the food to them. I could have never eaten all of it. But I did eat twice as much as usual, and I sure paid the price.

Sergeant Grant was waiting for me at the scullery, as I exited the mess hall. He knew I hadn't eaten all the food, but he didn't comment. He wasn't finished with me yet. When we got back to the barracks, he made me do one hundred push-ups and one hundred squat jumps for dessert.

"Private Iacampo, I hope you had enough to eat today?"

"Sir, yes sir."

I tried to keep the rest of my opinions to myself.

Chapter 19
Junk on the Bunk

Junk on the bunk was another form of harassment developed by some crackpot to annoy marines. It was not only done in boot camp, but was done from time to time during our regular enlistment. To make it simple, junk on the bunk is a clothing and equipment display, laid out in military fashion, on the bunk.

It was displayed in the most rigid fashion, according to the Marine Corps manual. All of your belongings had a specific place to be marked, covers, shirts, pants, underpants, undershirts, socks, shoes, boots, belts, and the rest. All marines had their equipment marked in the same place. The guidebook explained how to fold each piece of equipment and the measurements of it after it was folded. The blanket on the bunk had to be made so tight that a quarter could be bounced off of it. Just one more annoyance.

Hour after hour was spent on shining shoes and boots, washing and ironing clothing, and buffing brass. For the inspection your underwear had to be ironed. Socks had to be folded a certain way. If an Irish pennant (loose thread) was found anywhere on your belongings, the shit hit the fan. (I have no idea where the name Irish pennant came from.)

After hours of painstaking measures and preparation, all the clothing and equipment were laid out on the bunks for display.

The junk on the bunk took the better part of two days to

102

get ready. Everyone slept on the floor so the equipment could be placed on the bunk. The day of the inspection, all the recruits stood in front of their racks at attention. The DIs went through the displays with a fine-tooth comb. Sergeant Grant did the inspecting with a ruler in his hand. Sergeant Bail followed with a clipboard making notes. With all of the junk on the bunk inspections we had while in boot camp, not once did we pass inspection without some discrepancy.

The first inspection we had, the further Sergeant Grant got into the inspection, the madder he became. This was his nature. Before long all of the displays were on the floor in a big pile. He was like a mad dog tossing around a bone. Sergeant Bail stepped back and let him go. The displays took days to prepare and minutes to destroy. Some of the displays were so bad, in his opinion, that he dumped rack and all over. Everyone stood at attention while the madman was doing his thing.

"I don't know what the fuck is the matter with you shitheads. If the Marine Corps guidebook says your pants and covers are two inches apart, that's what it should be, not one inch, not three inches, but two inches." He found something wrong with every display. "We can keep this bullshit up all night, if that's what you shit birds want. Now you'd better get it right. Get your gear picked up and we will have another inspection in one hour. It best be right; now get your dead asses moving."

The first inspection took two days to prepare; now this one was supposed to be ready in one hour. God help us. It resembled a rummage sale at May Company. Everyone was pushing and shoving to get to their gear. Jackson and I banged heads in the process and just gave each other dirty looks. No time to beef.

The second and third inspections ended the same way as the first did, as catastrophes. Besides having all the displays thrown on the floor, we did calisthenics for good measure. This ordeal went into the early morning hours.

Chapter 20

The Other Troops

Private Wilmar was the only redneck I got along with in boot camp. He was a tall, lanky kid from the south with quite a personality. He could be described as a southern version of Ricky Nelson. He was about six-two, with bright red hair, good-looking and charming in his own way, with an enormous sense of humor. I often told him his daddy must have been Italian for him to have so much polish.

The only thing wrong with Wilmar, as far as I could see, was that he was an addict. He was addicted to Pepsi Cola.

On one of our morning runs around the island, at the other end of the base, Wilmar saw a Pepsi machine. That was his downfall. From that time on, that was all he could think of; he had to have a Pepsi. Most recruits have wet dreams, dreaming of their girl friends, or dream of getting out of boot camp. Not Wilmar. He was obsessed, he had to have that Pepsi. For weeks he formulated plans on how he was going to satisfy his desires. Wilmar and I were very close, and I was the only one to share in his secret. The more I heard about his plans, the crazier I told him he was. Anyone that would jeopardize his position at this point in boot camp was not playing with a full deck. I tried to talk him out of the mission impossible, but there was no changing this stump jumper's mind. The invasion of Normandy didn't take as much planning. He had to have a Pepsi.

The big night came one night after taps. Once again, I

tried to talk him out of this insanity. No way. About an hour after lights out, Wilmar made his move. I knew of his mission, so I was awake watching him leave the barracks. As he went by my rack, I whispered good luck, and told him he was fuckin' nuts. I was laughing so hard to myself and trying to keep it in, I thought I was going to piss my pants. He snuck out of the barracks like a dope fiend going to get a fix. *Mission Pepsi Cola was underway.*

The first part of his caper went without a hitch. He made it all the way to the Pepsi machine without being detected. He explained the scenario to me later on. He put the money in the machine and pushed the button, and out came an ice-cold Pepsi. He picked up the bottle and first caressed it like he would a "set of tits." He popped the top with a pocket knife he had and let that ice-cold Pepsi trickle down his throat. He thought that he had died and gone to heaven. "It sure was worth the risk."

When he fully recovered from his ecstasy, he began his trip back to the barracks. God only knows how he had gotten all the way there without someone on guard duty seeing him. Going back was different.

He got about a quarter of the way back and was challenged by a guard on patrol. "Halt, who goes there?" the guard called out. Wilmar, in all of his wisdom, thought he would trick the guard, and answered, "The corporal of the guard." The guard, being suspicious, called back to him, "Advance and be recognized." With that, the fleet-footed Wilmar began to run. He was extremely fast on his feet. He told me he was so fast from chasing all those hillbilly broads up and down the mountains. The second guard heard the first guard, the third heard the second, and so on. Before Wilmar knew it, he had most of the guard unit chasing him. He made it all the way back to the barracks without them actually catching him. They saw which barracks he ran into and followed him in there.

Naturally, everyone was sleeping, including Sergeant Grant, but not me; I was waiting to hear how everything went. I found out soon enough.

By the time Wilmar made it to the top of the stairs, the guard unit was right on his heels. Sergeant Grant was a light sleeper to start with. When he heard the commotion, he ran out of his quarters, half asleep and the other half pissed off for someone waking him up. As Wilmar turned the corner to run down the squad bay, Sergeant Grant latched on to him by his throat. "Jesus H. Christ, Wilmar. What the fuck is all the commotion about?" When he saw the guards, he knew that there was something really out of line.

Wilmar was really crapping in his pants. All of a sudden, he was having second and third thoughts about his adventure. In a meek tone of voice, he began to plead for his life. He told the good sergeant about his fantasy and his obsession with Pepsi. By that time nearly everyone in the squad bay was awake and listening to Wilmar pleading his case. Snickers could be heard all over the barracks, which pissed off Sergeant Grant even more. Wilmar's story was so convincing, he had me believing his line of shit.

"If I hear one more snicker out of you shit birds, I'll have you doing PT all night. Now shut the fuck up and hit the rack," Grant said.

Sergeant Grant dismissed the guard unit and ordered Wilmar to his quarters. Wilmar's only punishment for the caper was doing calisthenics the remainder of the night outside Sergeant Grant's quarters and running around the parade field, with his best friend, for two hours at a crack each day. I believe that if Sergeant Grant wasn't an alcoholic and didn't have similar desires, as far as booze went, he would have thrown the book at Wilmar. All in all, Wilmar got away with murder. He could have been court-martialed for what he had done.

Private Garrity was the platoon's strongman. He excelled in every physical fitness test given. He could do more one-handed push-ups than anyone I had ever seen. There wasn't anyone in the platoon or on the base that could match his strength. The black guys in the platoon called him "Cock-strong Garrity." "That boy must not have ever had a pussy to be that strong," they said and then everyone would laugh like hell.

King of the fleet feet was Private Hurrt. He was a black guy from one of the southern states whose feet went so fast, his body could barely keep up with them. Hurrt always represented 2028 in running competition with other platoons. He was always squared away, neat and clean, and made a good marine. He was about six-one and made a very good appearance in his uniform. With all those attributes, he was designated platoon "Guide-on," the person who carries the platoon's colors at the head of the formation. He had real rhythm in his steps and made the rest of the platoon look good.

Beside Hurrt and Jackson, there were three other black guys in the platoon. One of them was Private Hill. He was another sharp-looking, good marine. He and I had something in common. We were both from Cleveland and lived only a few miles from one another. Unlike the other guy from Cleveland, Private Hill never had a problem with Sergeant Grant. Hill knew when to talk and when not to talk.

Then there was Private George, dubbed Private Snowball by Sergeant Grant because he was so black. Sergeant Grant used to tell him, "Boy, when I talk to you, you'd better open your eyes and smile so I can see where your black ass is." The only correct response was "Sir, yes sir."

Jackson came from somewhere in New Jersey and thought he was a tough guy. He had all of the black guys in the platoon and some of the white guys afraid of him. A typical bully, he looked and talked tough, but I had run across lot of people like him where I grew up. He got his kicks pushing around guys that were smaller than he was. To top it off, he was a sloppy person. He always looked like had been on the back of a garbage truck all day. I didn't like the guy from the first time I bumped into him, and the feeling was mutual. It was in the stars that we would tangle.

Last of the black troops, but not the least, everyone's favorite, and Private Wayne's clone, was Private Green. On account of Wayne and Green, Platoon 2028 did four thousand more push-ups than we would have had to do if they weren't around. If both of their IQ's were combined, they wouldn't break 100. I still don't know how they passed their entrance exams to get into the Corps. Green and Wayne were so tall, Sergeant Grant would get on his tip-toes to chew their asses out.

"Boy, where the fuck are you from?"

"Alabama, sir," Green would answer.

"How tall are you, Alabama?"

"Six foot six, sir"

"I didn't know that shit could be stacked that high, boy. You are so full of shit, you got brown eyes, don't you, boy?"

Green had a smirk on his face, not knowing what to say or do.

"Boy, who the fuck are you smiling at? You'd better wipe that smile off your goddamn face before I do it for you, boy. Get down and give me fifty push-ups, or I'll kick your black ass all over this base."

Six weeks or so into basic training, everyone was taking the harassment of the noble tormentor more casually. A lot of the petty harassment started to taper off. For some of the internal problems that we had as a platoon, the platoon justice system was implemented. This saved a great deal of mass punishment. The less Sergeant Grant saw and the less he had to talk to us, the more peace and quiet we had. On several occasions, the smoke fiend Private Norris got out of line, and we took care of it, before the DIs became involved. This was the way the DIs wanted their platoon to eventually handle all their problems, as a unit. Just to keep the records straight, we were on the end of a smack from time to time. The green wienie never stopped.

Private Grace had two strikes against him before he came to PI. He couldn't adapt to military life, first because he was so dainty and second because his name was a definite anchor. "What the fuck happened to you, Grace? When you were born, did the Lord forget to give you a pussy? With a name like Grace, I would think that you would have a split between your legs." The verbal abuse kept up constantly with him. As soon as the DIs detect that a person is not fit for the Corps and there is a chance he is going to try to get out, the heat never stops. Grace made the unforgivable mistake of getting his parents involved with his boot camp problems. In turn, they got their congressman involved. Grace was trying to get a hardship discharge. To make a long story short, that meant for some reason he couldn't cut the service and was requesting a discharge, due to hardship. His parents wrote the congressman and told him how their son was getting abused in boot camp, and the congressman started making waves. The most annoying thing anyone can do to a DI is tell him how to run his platoon.

The word got to Sergeants Grant and Bail that Grace's congressman was stirring up trouble, and they began to apply PI heat.

Grace had only been in boot camp several weeks when his problem surfaced. Not only did he tell his parents the truth as to what was going on, but he exaggerated another hundred percent. Maybe he was only looking for sympathy, but he stirred up a can of worms. I have no idea why he ever joined the Marine Corps to start with. He didn't have any physical ability at all.

With the tight network PI is known for, it wasn't long before this boy's ass was in big trouble with the Gestapo.

"What's the matter, Grace? Did your mommy raise a fuckin' pussy? We don't allow pussies in my Marine Corps, boy. So you try your best to get the fuck out. In the meantime I am gonna bust your balls every way I can think of, so you remember your short stay here with us. From now on, boy, your ass is grass and I'm a fuckin' lawn mower. You couldn't make a pimple on a good marine's ass, so you'd better have your goddamn congressman get you the fuck out of my Corps." Sergeant Grant was at his best, foaming from the mouth right in Grace's face. "Now you'd better turn your head the other way; I can't stand lookin' at a fuckin' quitter."

The poor kid was having a nervous breakdown right then and there. "Sir, yes sir."

After the cat was let out of the bag about the congressman, Grace ceased to have any activities with the platoon, with the exception of chow. Between him and Parker, some of the heat was taken off the rest of us. They got every shit detail that came up. The minute one detail was finished, Grace or Parker was on another one.

"Grace, you belong at home with your mother washing floors. Do you think that your congressman gives two fucks about you? He's in Washington, D.C., having a good old time, and you got him to stick his nose in my business. You really piss me off, boy. Your mother better hurry and get her little pussy son out of my platoon, before I really kick his ass." (The worst thing Sergeant Grant could do was hit Grace, for sure then then Sergeant Grant sure would have had a problem.)

There was so much activity going on at that time in our training that no one paid too much attention to Grace. One day we discovered he was gone by his empty rack. No one ever asked.

Privates Coffey and Carraffa were born and raised in the same hometown: Waterbury, Connecticut. They went to the same schools and joined the Corps on the buddy plan. Carraffa was an Italian kid and naturally, I liked him immediately. He and Coffey were great kids. Carraffa and I made Coffey an honorary Italian, which we told him was quite a distinction. I was raised in the same kind of neighborhood they were, and we had a lot in common with each other. In the infancy stages of boot camp, we couldn't really communicate with one another that much. Later on, when the smoke cleared, we began enjoying each other's company. We used to sit around in our spare time, when we had spare time, and try to impress each other with our conquests of the opposite sex while in civilian life. Most of it was bullshit, but it made for good conversation. It was so amazing that the three of us were so much alike and I had lived so far away from where they did.

A fink is a fink is a fink (stool pigeon). An ass kisser is an ass kisser is an ass kisser (self-explanatory). Platoon 2028 had one such person in its ranks. His name was Caseman, Private (Fink Ass Kisser) Caseman. He was older than most of the rest of the platoon, maybe 23 or so. We considered that old for a recruit. Not a soul in the platoon had any use for him, not even Private (Smoke Fiend) Norris. Caseman probably had joined the Corps because he didn't have any friends on the outside. News flash: he didn't have any friends on the inside either. The wardens didn't even like him; they just used him as a snitch. They couldn't be with us twenty-four hours a day, so they had to have someone on the inside let them know what was going on. When the platoon finally figured out that Caseman was the informer, he was blacklisted. From that day on, no one had anything to do with him. What a price to pay. Aside from being a fink, he had a face only a mother could love, maybe. When we busted his balls, we used to tell him his mother had to tie a pork chop round his neck so the family dog would play with him, he was so ugly. To repay him for being a snitch, the DIs made him a squad leader, trying to enhance his popularity. It didn't work. No one could put a hand on Caseman for fear of getting in a jackpot with Sergeant Grant. We had to bide our time. Eventually, we would get him.

Private Curlis was one of the most celebrated people in the platoon, as far as the recruits were concerned, because of one unusual characteristic. When the pressures of boot camp slowed up, he used to wake up every morning with an erection, having had a wet dream during the night. There were several occasions when he woke up and his sheet was stuck to his penis. He had to run down the squad bay and into the head before he was seen by one of our guardians. It was quite a sight. One morning, his luck ran out and he got caught, let's say, red-handed.

"Private Curlis, what the fuck you got in that sheet, boy?"

"Sir, I had an accident, and I am going to the head to take care of it."

"Curlis, you'd better hurry the fuck up. If I ever catch you playing with that accident, you got big problems, boy!"

In one of our bullshitting sessions, Curlis told us the reason he was in the Corps was because he had knocked up some young girl and had to get out of town.

The television series "Gomer Pyle, USMC" could have been made years before it was and starred Platoon 2028's Private Trail. This guy looked and acted more like Gomer Pyle than Gomer Pyle did. The only thing he didn't do that Gomer did was say, "Golly-ee." The similarity between the two was uncanny. Trail walked like Pyle, talked like Pyle, and looked like Pyle. He was another stump jumper that had to have someone forge his papers to get into the service.

Platoon 2028 had two people named Morris and Morres.

First and best was the house mouse Morris. He was such a likable little guy, everyone adopted him as their younger brother. If he had told me he was thirteen years old, I would have believed him. He just barely made all the minimum requirements to get into the Corps. His duties were to run all the errands for the DIs. Getting the cigarettes when the smoking lamp was lit and getting the mail for the platoon were just two of his assignments. Not once that I could remember did he get into trouble with Sergeant Grant.

And then there was the big fat kid whose name was Morres. He escaped getting in the Fat Man's Platoon by the skin of his teeth. His father must have been a friend of someone in the military. No one else in Morres's condition could have made it through boot camp the way he did. He was one of the recruits that had to be pulled along when the running became extreme. Going through the confidence course, he had to be pushed over the walls that we were to scale. Climbing a thirty-foot rope was out of the question; he never got four feet off the ground. Everything he attempted was a massive struggle. All the while that he was battling every obstacle, Sergeant Grant was on his ass yelling and screaming. He sure had to have some political pull that no one else had. It never dawned on me that he may have been Sergeant Grant's nephew or something. At the end of thirteen weeks of basic training, there was some noticeable improvement in him but not much. The thing I resented most about Morres—beside the fact I just didn't care for him—was that I was the one who usually had to carry or drag him along. He was like trying to pull a Sherman tank.

Private Langer might have been Gomer Pyle and Private Trail's cousin. His ears stuck out so far, he looked like a taxicab with the door open. Sergeant Grant got into his face about those big ears several times. "Private Langer, there is one thing you never have to worry about."

"What is that, sir?" Langer replied.

"Your cover will never fall over your eyes, boy. I have never seen a set of ears like yours in my life, boy. I am gonna call you Private Dumbo."

Langer was the only person in the platoon that had a harder time learning to march than the black and white clones Green and Wayne. He looked just like a robot when he walked. His gait was 25 percent slower than the rest of the platoon. After thousands of push-ups and squat jumps, Sergeant Grant had Sergeant Bail give him private lessons, trying to get him to march correctly.

Private Dimple was named very appropriately. There was a dimple in his chin so big, a bus could be parked in it.

"Boy, if your chin had some hair on it, it would look just like a pussy. Did anyone ever try and get some of that chin, huh, boy?" In simple terms, Sergeant Grant had the most morbid and crudest sense of humor of anyone I ever met. He took a shot at everyone. Sergeant Bail never had a reaction to any of his boss's nonsense.

The brains of the platoon was Private Orr. He used to tutor all of the recruits that were having difficulty reading or writing. It was obvious Orr came from a good background. He was polished and had a lot of character. I would have thought he would have stayed a civilian and gone to college and gotten a good education. Maybe somewhere down the road he finished his education in the Corps.

Edwards was one of the recruits that received a Dear John letter from his girlfriend when he was in boot camp. Most of the guys just shook off getting Dear John letters as part of the game. Edwards went into the head one night after mail call and tried to shave his wrists with a dull blade. It's a good thing he did it in the shower as the blood was a lot easier to clean up there. People that pulled shots like that never came back

115

from sick bay. They were immediately shipped out and given a medical discharge.

Three barracks down from ours was a big black DI that was wackier in some ways than Sergeant Grant and had a disposition to match. As the tale goes, he had a thing for sandbags. Anyone in his platoon that messed up had two full sandbags slung over his shoulder and ran laps around the parade field. (It seemed like each senior DI tried to outdo his counterparts with a nastier punishment.) One day, one of Sergeant Sandbag's recruits did something out of line. Sergeant Sandbag made him run the parade route routine. On one of his trips around the parade ground, the kid either flipped or had it planned, but he charged the DI, whose back was turned, and put a bayonet between his shoulder blades. Sergeant Sandbag went to the big kitty litter box in the sky. The recruit was brought up on murder charges, naturally found guilty, and put in prison. There had to have been many confrontations between the two of them before that occurred, and the recruit had all he could take.

Chapter 21
Looking Better

Time was clicking by at a very rapid pace now. The platoon was on the downward side of boot camp, and things were looking better all the time. The change from harassment to harmony began to take place. It seemed like one morning we woke up to the chimes of the pounding of the iron pipe, but it didn't faze us anymore, and the sun was shining in the squad bay. The pounding now sounded like tapping. Things were surely improving. I can't say it was a pleasure to be on PI, but I can say it was a vast improvement from where we had been. Platoon 2028 started to qualify as a Marine Corps platoon. The long, hard hours we spent drilling and marching showed miraculous results. We now were proud of what we had accomplished.

On several occasions we were able to compete with other platoons in touch football and track events. In touch football particularly, we had a chance to expend some of our pent-up energy and aggression.

During one such activity, Private Jackson and I finally locked horns. This was about two months in the waiting. The scrimmage was being played within the platoon. Jackson and I were on opposite teams, which made the contest even more enjoyable. During one of his O. J. Simpson moves to the goal line, I clotheslined him. I knew it was not exactly a legal maneuver, but it worked: he didn't make the touchdown. One of the major principles we were taught at PI was to win at all

117

costs. I always had a competitive attitude anyway, so hitting Jackson was a natural instinct. When he got his butt off the ground, he started swinging wildly at me without saying a word, but never making contact. I countered with a few of my own before Sergeant Grant stepped in between us. I was laughing at Jackson, which pissed him off more.

"I know you two assholes have been waiting to kick the shit out of each other for a long time, so I am gonna give you the chance. When we get back to the barracks, we'll settle this," Sergeant Grant said.

In between the barracks, bets were being made with cigarettes and poggy bait (candy). Sergeant Grant directed the house mouse to his quarters to get two pairs of boxing gloves he had for just such occasions. The odds on the fight were being made in my favor, although Jackson had some support. He was big and slow; I was lean and mean. There was no doubt in my mind what the outcome of the fight was going to be.

"You two shit birds have been eyeballing each other for a long time. There isn't anything that goes on in my platoon I don't know about. I want you to settle this once and for all," the sergeant told us.

When the bell rang, I wouldn't exactly call it a professional fight. Jackson hit me, I hit him, and it went back and forth. During the contest he tried to hit me with a roundhouse punch. I blocked it and kicked him right in the balls. That also was illegal but also worked. I followed that up with two punches to the face, and that was the name of that tune. The altercation lasted about three minutes, with me getting the definite edge. Although my nose was bleeding, I gave him a fatter lip and a blacker eye than he was born with. The troops were cheering wildly; winning or losing a pack of cigarettes was a big deal. By the time the contest reached its climax, I was declared the winner by our referee, Sergeant Grant. I must admit Jackson was a good opponent. Oddly enough, we never had another cross word with one another for the duration of our training. We sort of became allies.

Now all of the deadweight had been eliminated from the platoon: the overweight people, slashers, would-be gays and quitters. All in all about ten people that started with us never finished with us. The pride of the Corps had done their jobs well. The brainwashing and the indoctrination had made their mark. After almost two and one-half months of training, boot camp became sort of a job now, instead of a sentence. I never thought I would see the day when we were allowed to go to the outdoor theater, be able to have more than three smokes a day, and basically be treated almost like human beings, always bearing in mind we still didn't want to piss off Sergeant Grant; he still was lord and master.

The giant medicine ball game was another game we played to vent our anger. The ball was about four feet round, made of heavy canvas, and filled with rags. The object of the game was for one team to get the ball past the other team's goal line, by any means possible. There were no rules to the game, and it resembled unorganized rugby. Now was the time for some of the disliked recruits to get their reward. They could have their asses kicked legally.

Sides were chosen. Most of my friends were on my team. It was a coincidence that Caseman and Norris happened to be on the opposing team. Sergeant Grant and Sergeant Bail were the referees, there to enforce the rules, which did not exist. They knew before the game started what the outcome was going to be: get-even time. All in all, they disliked the finks and troublemakers more than we did. Very little attempt was made to score points.

Let the games begin. Wilmar, Carraffa, Coffey, Hill, and Hard Dick Curlis were on my team. Jackson was the captain of the other team, but he knew what our objective was. We didn't care if we won or lost the game; the plan was to get the smoke fiend and the fink. We pushed the ball to them deliberately, so we could pound the shit out of them. They were getting hit from every direction; we were just trying to get Caseman and Norris. They were catching more elbows, fists, and knees than they would have in a bar fight. By the time the whistle blew, those two guys were a sight for sore eyes. Caseman was looking in Sergeant Grant's direction for sympathy but wasn't getting any. Norris knew better. Sergeant Bail had been laughing his ass off during the game. Sergeant Grant didn't crack a smile. The smoke fiend and the fink had their day in court. Guilty as charged.

The pugil sticks were another innovation of Marine Corps boot camp. They were sticks about four feet long, padded on each end. The stick was supposed to be a simulated rifle, with a bayonet on the end. This was not a game we played, but an exercise in how to use a rifle and bayonet in combat. The two combatants were equipped with gloves and helmets.

Before the competition began, we were given a crash course by a buck sergeant on the use of this make-believe weapon. This sergeant taught this course as one of his assignments. Most of the hotshot instructors tried to show you how good they were, instead of demonstrating the technique properly, and ours was no exception. In giving his demonstration, he called in two recruits to show off with, me being one of them.

"This is a simulated rifle with a bayonet at the top. It is held in the following fashion. It will be used in this manner," the instructor lectured. With that he proceeded to beat the hell out of me and one other recruit, showing off his so-called talent.

The standing rule in Platoon 2028 was that Private Iacampo was always the guinea pig, always up first. I was first in the ring with Private Morres. Just from getting my ass kicked by the instructor I was in a nasty mood. As the contest between Morres and me began I grabbed the end of the apparatus, swung it over my head like a baseball bat, hit Morres right in the head, and knocked him down.

The enraged instructor ran over to me, grabbed the pugil stick out of my hands, and began to yell, "What the fuck is the matter with you, boy? Don't you know that you just grabbed the bayonet and cut the shit out of your hands? That is not the way you are to use this weapon; this is!" And again he proceeded to pound me with it. Lesson seventy-two. But at least I got a chance to get a whack at the fat boy.

Chapter 22

Guard Duty

Among the more unpleasant and monotonous chores at PI was guard duty. It was another facet of our training that everyone had to go through to prepare for combat situations. This part of our training took place when the platoons were on the downhill side of boot camp.

A dozen or so posts were set around the base, most of which were very low security areas, just to have the recruits get used to the responsibility of guard duty. Some of the areas were empty buildings, gates that went nowhere, and even dumpsters.

The shifts were set up around the clock, in four-hour increments, with eight hours off in between shifts. Time off was spent cleaning rifles, studying general orders, sleeping, or doing whatever else we wanted to do before our next watch came up. This tour of duty lasted one week. The only good thing about guard duty was that we didn't see the DIs for the whole week. The activities of the recruits on guard duty were controlled by permanent personnel.

While we were on duty, our appearance was of utmost importance. Rifles had to be cleaned, with the stocks highly buffed. Shoes and boots had to be shined, and uniforms had to be cleaned and ironed. Inspections while on duty were commonplace. Smoking at the post was not allowed.

At any given time, the post might be inspected by the corporal of the guard or the officer of the day. One of their motives for checking the posts was to make sure the person on duty was manning the post correctly, not sleeping or smoking, but knowing what guard duty represented. Along with being alert, the sentry had to know his general orders (ten of them) and what his duties were for guarding this specific location. Quite often the person checking the post would park his vehicle a good distance from the post to try to surprise the sentry.

As most posts were in isolated areas, guard duty was very boring, just walking back and forth for hours at a time. The temptation was very great for someone to go to sleep or smoke to break the monotony. Everyone was aware of the penalty for these infractions, but some people did take the chance. Some got away with it, others didn't.

Private Young was one of the unlucky people that got caught. All through his basic training, he never got into any trouble and virtually went unnoticed. While on guard one night, Young became tired and sat down on a box to relax. The corporal of the guard sneaked up on him and caught him sleeping. He was put on report and had office hours with the company commander. He tried to be up front with the CO and told him he had sat down to rest and fallen asleep. His honesty was what saved him from a more severe penalty. He was sent to another platoon and had one additional month to serve at PI. I wonder if the nap was worth the penalty. He could have been sent to the brig and court-martialed. All of our training was done to prepare us for actual combat situations. If someone fell asleep in combat, it could cost the life of everyone in the platoon or company.

There was always someone trying to beat the system. Tricks were passed on from platoon to platoon. One of the tricks was, if a person wanted to get some shuteye but not sleep too long, they would sit down in a comfortable spot out of the view of anyone, light a cigarette, and fall asleep. When the cigarette would burn all the way down, it would burn their fingers, and they would wake up. Getting caught smoking on guard duty was bad enough, but getting caught smoking *and* sleeping was double trouble. None of the people in Platoon 2028 were ever caught, but I heard of some others that were. To me, it would hardly be worth all that effort.

For safety precautions, our rifles didn't have any ammo in them. Needless to say, some of these guys were dangerous enough without a loaded weapon. The areas we were guarding were not critical; this was just for training purposes. It's a good thing that ammo was not issued. The duty was so boring that sometimes your imagination would run away with you. You would see things and hear things that didn't exist. If some of the recruits did have live ammo, half of the guard unit would have been shot.

Weather conditions were not a factor while on duty. Rain or shine, twenty-four hours a day the posts were manned. If the weather was favorable, keeping squared away for duty wasn't bad. If it rained, keeping your uniform and rifle in good condition took a lot of extra work. When a rifle got wet, it had to be disassembled completely, cleaned, oiled, and put back together. Rifle inspection while on duty was a common practice. Uniforms had to be cleaned and pressed at all times. The ten general orders for guard duty had to be memorized and applied if someone checked the post.

Chapter 23
Daily Activities

In the military being self-sufficient was of the utmost importance. Some of the recruits in Platoon 2028 had never made a bed or scrubbed a floor before coming to boot camp. In addition to keeping our personal hygiene in order, which some of the troops found annoying at first, it was the responsibility of each recruit to wash and iron his clothes. We also had to clean the heads and the barracks, top to bottom, and the outside area around the barracks. Many people found it difficult getting into the routine, because their parents had done everything for them when they were home. Most everyone adjusted without incident. When someone was stubborn, platoon justice took over.

One recruit from day one had a tough time getting into the rain room. When the DIs were on our back at first, he had no choice. As soon as conditions became better for the platoon, he slacked off on his showers. It was the unanimous (minus one, of course) opinion of the platoon that if Fells naphtha soap and scrub brushes worked so well getting clothes clean, they should work well on Private Crud. One night when he was lying on his rack and was supposed to be in the rain room, about four of the platoon enforcers dragged him to the shower and gave him what is called a GI shower. Sergeant Bail was on duty that night and was in his quarters but didn't pay attention to the commotion. I think he knew what was going on.

In between the barracks were concrete scrub racks, with running water, where we did our laundry by hand. These racks were shared by multiple platoons, mainly the people next door. Three to four times a week, we would hand scrub all of our clothes and hang them out to dry. After our clothes dried, we ironed everything from covers to skivvies.

I would always look for a shortcut, trying to preserve time and do things the easy way. There were two pairs of skivvies that I used over and over. The rest I kept ironed and folded, in case there was a surprise junk on the bunk. I would wear a pair all day, that night wear them into the shower and scrub them while showering, dry them out overnight, and the next day repeat the same process. When that pair wore out, I would throw them away and use two other sets.

The shine on a marine's shoes will tell you what kind of marine he is. Hour upon hour was spent spit-shining shoes and boots. One trick to getting a better shine was to set the polish on fire to burn out the alcohol. After the flame was extinguished, it gave the wax an additional benefit, giving the shine the greatest luster. Some crackpot marine probably came up with that idea, and we followed it.

Mail call was an occasion that everyone really looked forward to. Getting a letter from home was a real morale booster in most cases. But for some of the recruits, they received more bad news than good. When a person is down and out to start with and receives bad news, especially in a letter, it has a great impact on them. Private Edwards was one example. He slit his wrist over a Dear John letter he got. His case was one of the more drastic.

Even better than getting good news from home was getting a care package (with goodies inside). We were not allowed to get any packages for the first two months of basic training. Most of the things we got from home were things that were unavailable at the PX (post exchange). Most everyone received cookies, pastries, and things of that nature.

A Manners Big Boy (double decker hamburger) was the item I craved the most while at PI. In my letters I asked my mother if she could send me one. Instead she sent me something I loved even better, which wouldn't spoil. We will call it an Italian care package. It had salami, capacola, three different kinds of cheese, sausage, and a few other Italian delicacies.

The package was wrapped in a way that only a good Italian could, with four rolls of accumulated twine and three rolls of used newspaper, then wrapped in heavy duty shipping paper.

The day I got the package, I was ecstatic, though I had no idea what was in it. Sergeant Grant and the house mouse were conducting mail call. As soon as I got the package, I ran to my footlocker, sat down, and began to open it. As soon as I pierced the outside wrapper, I knew what was inside. The aroma filled the barracks immediately. It had taken about two weeks for the package to arrive, so all of its contents were very ripe. "Jesus H. Christ, Iacampo, what the fuck is in that package? It smells like something I would fuck." Sergeant Grant didn't have any class. But this time I didn't pay attention to half the things he said. "My feet don't smell that bad, boy. Is there something dead in that package? You'd better do something with it, boy: you are smelling up my whole base."

"Sir, yes sir."

"If you're gonna eat whatever is in that package, you'd better get started, and get it the fuck out of my squad bay: go outside behind the barracks with it."

"Sir, yes sir."

I got together with Carraffa and Coffey and we had a feast. We took a Cabar (military knife) and scraped all the mold off (free penicillin), sliced everything up and chowed down. I invited Wilmar to join us, but he refused. He said his stomach wasn't strong enough. Private Jackson's comment was, "You fuckin' Italians gotta have guts like cast iron." He laughed like hell. He was my buddy now.

It was great getting the care package, but like most things, we paid the price for eating all those highly seasoned, fat-filled goodies. The grease and the hot South Carolina sun don't mix too well. That afternoon we had a five-mile run. Carraffa, Coffey, and I were so green we looked like Martians. But it was well worth it.

Chapter 24
Confidence Course

All of our training really began to come together. We became comfortable with just about everything we did. For the most part, the Corps was in our veins.

The confidence course was next in line for our training, very well named, due to its complexity. It was set up quite a distance from the barracks in a semi-wooded area. All of the obstacles were designed to simulate different impediments that might be encountered in a combat situation. There were walls to scale, ropes to climb, cargo nets to go up and over, ponds that had to be crossed by using slings or ropes, horizontal telephone poles and ladders to cross, and trails to run. A stop watch was used to time us as we went through most of the obstacles.

At the beginning and end of each obstacle, Sergeants Grant and Bail were cheering us on. "Come on you bunch of pussies! My mother is in better shape than you are!" I almost knew what Sergeant Grant was going to say before he said it. "You couldn't make a pimple on a good marine's ass, Private Morres. Let's hurry and get that fat ass of yours over the wall. We don't have all fuckin' day to wait for you. I might be too old to eat before you get through this course, Morres. Let's get with it." Each and every time Morres barely made it. I think he was too dense for all the verbal abuse he took. He always had a blank, stupid look on his face.

There was one obstacle I remember most vividly. Two

telephone poles were on either side of a pond of water about ten to twelve feet deep. A guide wire went from one pole to the other. One pole was about four and a half feet off the ground; the other one was about twenty feet high. On the twenty-foot pole there were rungs to climb to the top, with a small platform near the top. When the recruit climbed to the top of the pole, he sat on the platform and wrapped his legs around the guide wire and grabbed on with his hands. Then, hand over hand, he made his way down to the pole on the other side of the pond. Sounds simple.

As in everything else Platoon 2028 did, Iacampo was the first one to try it. I was never afraid of heights, so climbing the pole was no big deal. I sat on the platform, grabbed the guide wire with my legs and hands, and began to make my way over the pond. About halfway across, I felt someone shaking the wire, looked down, and saw Sergeant Grant and Sergeant Bail on the other end of the wire trying to shake me off. For some reason, that day I had worn my low quarter boots, and the wire was cutting into my ankles. I stopped and tried to regroup while Laurel and Hardy were having their fun. When they stopped shaking the wire, I began to go down again. They did that about four or five times. Each time I would let go with my feet and hang there by my hands. Sergeant Bail was laughing his head off; Stone Face wasn't cracking a smile. I knew they wouldn't be happy unless I fell off into the water. About the sixth time they shook the wire, I released the wire with my legs, hung there for a second, and dropped into the water. I had no idea how deep the water was, but I went down about ten feet and hit the bottom with my feet. I quickly got my feet out of the mud and came to the surface. I didn't see anyone jumping in to help me. When I surfaced, Sergeant Bail was still laughing, and Sergeant Grant chewed me out for falling into the water. "Iacampo, you are a real pussy. You can't even hold onto a little wire. Hurry up, get your fuckin' ass back up that pole and try it again."

The second try ended with the same results, only this time they shook the wire more violently. "Come on, Iacampo; you're supposed to be one of those badasses. Let's try it once more." I was their entertainment for that day. The third time, without them shaking the wire, I made it to the bottom with no problem.

I wasn't the only one they harassed, but they worked on me the most. Each and every night I still got the green wienie, either the concrete weights drill or getting dropped by my surrogate father. It seems hard to believe, but a person can even get used to getting hit after a while.

The rest of the confidence course was fun. By now, 99 percent of the troops could handle anything that came down the pike. But the best was yet to come.

The last obstacle we had to contend with was the infiltration course. While live .30-caliber ammo was being fired over our heads, we had to crawl under barbed wire with our rifles and packs, through the mud and slop. Two machine guns were mounted at the end of the course in concrete blocks, facing in the direction we had to crawl. I don't know exactly how far over our heads the ammo was, but I dragged my nose from one end of the course to the other. At the sides of the course, the good sergeants were there cheering us on with words of encouragement. "You'd better keep your fuckin' heads down, ladies; you won't have anything to put your covers on. This is what it's like for real. You want to be marines; you'd better start acting like marines." Some of the recruits freaked out and stopped in the middle; the live ammo was too much for them. The sergeants encouraged them as follows: "You pussies better keep moving. If I have to come in there and get you, you're gonna be sorry. Green, if you don't keep your black ass moving, I'm gonna get on the machine gun myself and shoot your ass full of holes." By the time Green got to the other end, he was about two shades lighter. After the third or fourth time, everyone made it through with no problem.

I don't know how true it is, but I heard that over the years several people got hit with stray bullets and one or more died as a result of this training.

Each day when we completed different parts of the course, an overhaul of our rifles and gear was necessary. Inspections were given at random to make sure no one was slipping up.

Chapter 25
The Rifle Range

Going to the rifle range in boot camp meant that the platoon was really salty (had been around awhile). Graduation was not far off, something everyone awaited anxiously.

For two months, we had slept with our rifles, cleaned them, oiled them, and shined them, we had learned how to assemble and disassemble them blindfolded, and now we were going to get to shoot them. Our best friends were going to make some smoke.

Safety was the biggest consideration given when using the rifle. A lot of time was spent on teaching us to load and unload the weapons. Safety lesson number one: Never point a loaded or unloaded weapon at anyone unless you intend to shoot him. Many a recruit got the shit slapped out of him for pointing a rifle at someone. This was the only time I would agree with hitting a recruit. Quite a few people have been shot at the rifle range, accidentally or on purpose, through the years. It wouldn't be hard for someone who had it in for a DI to even the score here. It would be a perfect alibi at the rifle range.

The M-1 rifle was the weapon used by the marines in 1958. It was a clip-fed semi-automatic rifle, as I said earlier. A small part in the trigger mechanism that kept the rifle from firing automatically was called a sear. An automatic weapon will keep firing as long as the trigger is held down and the weapon has ammo. A semi-automatic weapon will only fire one round at a time.

There were three different distances that were used for qualification: two hundred, three hundred, and five hundred yards. At the two-hundred-yard line, the rifle was fired from the offhand position (standing). At the three-hundred-yard line, it was fired from the sitting position. At the five-hundred-yard line, it was fired from the prone position (lying down on your stomach).

Instructions were given on the correct way to fire the weapon: Take aim, breathe deeply, exhale slowly, and squeeze the trigger. Squeeze, never pull, the trigger. It is critical never to move after taking aim. If the muzzle of the rifle was moved one inch while on the five-hundred-yard line, its round would miss the target by more than ten feet.

I'd heard the expression *Kentucky windage* before but never seen it applied until I saw some of the hillbillies shoot. If there was anything they excelled in, it was shooting. They had a unique way of shooting the rifle without using the preferred Marine Corps method, but with great accuracy. Wilmer said he learned to play with his rifle before he played with himself. To most of the good old boys, firing a rifle was easier than falling off a log. Kentucky windage must have been a hillbilly secret, or they didn't know how to explain it. They wouldn't or couldn't explain how they used it. Most of the stump jumpers qualified as Expert Riflemen at the rifle range.

The area where the targets were located was called the butts. It was a long concrete bunker with an open top, and large mounds of dirt and grass in front of it. There were about a dozen targets, four feet square, in the bunkers, all chain-driven, and each one was manned by recruits who pulled them up and down manually.

A rotation of recruits was set up that pulled up the targets up and down, placing spotters on the targets to indicate where the target was hit. Live ammo could be heard flying overhead while we were in the bunkers, spotting targets; it couldn't have been more than ten feet away. An observation I made after the fact: One of the reasons the military is so successful with their discipline and people following orders is that 85 percent of the recruits in the service were under the age of twenty. The fear of God was put into each of them from day one. There wasn't anything that Sergeant Grant told me to do that I would have questioned, because of my young age and inexperience in life and his intimidation. They had no room for people that rationalized. "Respond without thought" was their motto.

If I were in my late twenties or early thirties, there was no way that I would have crawled under barbed wire with machine-gun fire four feet over my head or pulled targets with live ammo flying so close by with no head cover. Here, as in the infiltration course, there were several accidents over the years, with people getting hit by stray bullets. This was not a safe place.

After each group fired at the targets, time was called and the people in the butts pulled down the targets and placed spotters in the bullet holes. Black spotters went in the white areas of the target, and white spotters went in the black areas. Then the targets were pushed back up so the shooters could see where they had hit, and score was kept. We could actually stand there and watch the rounds going into the paper targets. From time to time a bullet would hit the metal part of the frame and ricochet. Where the bullet went no one knew. We were too young and stupid to even think of the danger.

All of the commands at the rifle range were given over the loudspeaker, to minimize confusion and ensure everyone heard the instructions.

"Lock and load: all ready on the right; all ready on the left; all ready on the firing line; watch your targets; targets." When the last command, "targets," was given, the people in the bunkers pushed the targets up and the people on the firing line commenced firing. When the allotted time was up a whistle blew and the targets were pulled down and marked. They were then pushed back up so the scores could be kept. After a week of shooting, scores were compiled and tabulated. The three categories of qualifying were Expert, Sharpshooter, and Marksman.

It was not uncommon for someone to turn away from the targets with a loaded weapon, not thinking. When that happened, either a DI or someone attached to the range immediately pounced on the person. It happened almost to every group that went through the rifle range, and Platoon 2028 was no exception. Private Peters, after loading his rifle, not thinking, turned to ask Sergeant Bail a question. Sergeant Bail screamed at the top of his lungs, and Peters got shook up and pulled the trigger, shooting a round in the air. When Private Peters emerged from the bottom of the pile of DIs and range personnel, he had the imprint of the rifle in his forehead. He spent the rest of the day running around the rifle range with his weapon at port arms. It was very lucky no one got shot.

It was necessary to qualify with three weapons at this range, the M-1, the BAR (Browning automatic rifle), and the .45 pistol.

On one particular day, we were practicing with the BAR. Wilmar was in the bunker alongside me. When he wasn't looking, I put his cover on a black spotter and stuck the spotter in the target. When the command "targets" was given, I ran the target up with his cover attached. The bullets were ripping the cover apart as the other recruits fired the BAR. From the firing line they couldn't see the cover; all they could see was the target. I poked him in the side and motioned for him to look up. When he did, he started to laugh like hell, not knowing the cover was his. When I pulled the target down, the cover was literally destroyed, except for the name on the brim.

I took it off and handed it to him. The laughing stopped and the cussing began. He called me everything he could think of. We had a good laugh about it, and I gave him forty-five cents for a new hat. We needed something to break the monotony that day.

The last weapon that we were required to qualify with was the .45 pistol. It was a very inaccurate weapon shot at a distant target, but very powerful and accurate at close range.

During and following our stay at the rifle range, living conditions became bearable. We were no longer considered sub–human beings all the time. For the first time since we became wards of the Marine Corps, we had the liberty to talk to someone without first getting permission. It felt great. More and more freedoms were given to us, a little at a time. We were now allowed to carry cigarettes with us and smoke in designated areas, where there were no restrictions. We must have died and gone to heaven. Some of the liberties we had taken for granted before were being given back to us. Not having someone leaning over your shoulder twenty-four hours a day was a big relief. Still there was the pock-faced DI lurking behind the scenes, waiting for someone to screw up so he could keep his devious ways honed. We could never relax 100 percent.

On one particular day at the rifle range we fell out for PT. For some reason, I was in an agitated mood. About two weeks earlier, 2028 had picked up a little five-foot, three-inch, built-like-a-brick-shithouse, mean-as-a-junkyard-dog DI named Sergeant Davis. The chip on his shoulder was about as high as he was tall. A person could tell that Davis was just waiting for someone to give him a bad time. We heard through the grapevine he had gotten into some trouble with another platoon and was laying low with 2028 for a while. Cover-ups in the Corps were not unheard of. As we were doing PT, I mumbled something under my breath like "son of a bitch."

He heard me from about twenty feet away. He must have had sonar in his ears. He ran over and cold-cocked me while we were doing squat jumps. I slid across the dew-covered grass like a rocket. Some of the other recruits told me it looked like I was water-skiing on my back. He didn't know that I had one of the better jaws around and could take a good punch. He ran over to where I stopped skidding and straddled me. "Private, you'd better never cuss at me again, or I'll kick your fuckin' ass all over the island. Do you read me, boy?"

"Sir, yes sir." I believed him, too.

This little guy had a chip on his shoulder with everyone, even the other DIs. I never saw him talk to anyone except in the line of duty.

When the platoon got back to main side (where our regular barracks were), Davis was roughing up Coffey in the hallway between the barracks. Down the hallway in the other barracks was a first lieutenant inspecting the other platoon. He saw Sergeant Davis bouncing Coffey off the walls and put Davis on report. (Where the hell was this lieutenant when Sergeant Grant was using me for a punching bag all those months?) The sergeant was court-martialed, busted, and transferred off Parris Island.

When we were sent to Camp Geiger in North Carolina for infantry training after basic training, I saw Sergeant Davis, now Corporal Davis. I never said a word to him; I didn't know if he saw me or not. I just kept walking.

The duty we had on the rifle range was the best duty we had so far, since coming to PI.

Our daily routine had become fairly consistent now, as far as drilling and the PT went. By this time everyone in the platoon, with the exception of fat Morres, was in the best condition of their lives. Platoon 2028 was considered one of the top-notch platoons on the island, as far as our marching skills and physical conditioning went. We could and did compete with the best platoon at PI and beat them. Our confidence was at an all-time high. We started to feel like marines, and that was what we came here for.

Chapter 26

Mess Duty

As the old saying goes, what goes around comes around. Now we were on the other side of the mess line serving the new recruits that had just been sentenced to death row. Was it possible that two and a half months ago we looked as bad and pathetic as these guys did? The expressions on their faces were ones of sheer terror. I couldn't imagine we looked that bad. I sort of felt sorry for them. I was always a sympathetic person. I remembered when I stood on the other side of that line, didn't know my ass from first base, and was fearing for my life. (I never have before and never have since experienced the fear I had in my body the first week of boot camp. It was indescribable.) I served them in a civil fashion, but some of the would-be badasses slung the food at them in a very immature manner. Private Norris was born a maggot and was still a maggot. When he was serving the new recruits, he would say, "Who you lookin' at, boy?" trying to reinforce his small ego. I was going to slap the shit out of him, but by now I was tired of beating him up. I did tell him several times to leave the new kids alone, but he was a small-time punk who got his rocks off picking on less fortunate people.

The system at PI was set up so when the rifle range duty was over, the platoon went right on mess duty. The jobs on mess duty varied, from peeling potatoes to washing dishes, serving the troops, or cleaning the mess hall after chow. Most of the jobs were rotated during the week of duty. None of the duty was bad. We knew that in a matter of weeks we would be graduating and getting off Paradise Island.

One of the benefits of being on mess duty was getting all the food and all the cold milk we wanted. I used to drink five or six glasses of milk at a meal.

During one of my trips into the meat locker, I noticed the stamp on the meat that was hanging was GRADE B, a low quality of meat. I was really surprised. I thought the military always served its troops high-grade meat. It could be that the purchasing agent was getting his palm greased, taking the money for Grade A and buying Grade B. A lot of people got rich in the military who had control of purchasing in one department or another.

Chapter 27
Almost There

For the most part we now were no longer referred to as maggots by Sergeant Grant. When the warden wasn't pissed off at something or someone, he began to address us as "you people this" and "you people that." I was shocked the first time he referred to us in that manner, as I was waiting for the punch line. Things were getting so civilized that I was expecting the boom to fall at any time. These conditions were not normal or what we had been used to.

Living conditions were at least 1000 percent better than they had been. We went from the dregs of hell halfway to civilization.

Sergeant Grant didn't completely reform. On a regular basis he would still run off at the mouth. By now we were used to him. Good old Sergeant Bail just followed the boss around, still trying to look mean. The impact the DIs had on their recruits was remarkable and long-lasting. If a time of war existed, the DI would go into combat with the platoon after basic training was completed. This would keep the edge on the troops to follow orders without hesitation. That is what it was all about, undying loyalty to the Corps.

We had a few more junk on the bunks and one more shower drill, just to keep the pressure on us. We could handle anything at this point. We knew it wouldn't be long before we were getting our walking papers from this place. We could now see the light at the end of the tunnel, only now it wasn't a train coming at us. Most of us took all the shit they threw at us and survived. Some people went through boot camp almost unnoticed, and others, like me, really tested the system. I don't think I could have done it any differently. PI was the biggest challenge I had ever been confronted with in my life. I had to see for myself just how far I could go. It was a lot more than I could have ever dreamed of or bargained for. I was born testing the system, and I probably will die the same way. Although I never learned to conform completely, I became better with age.

We were now allowed to smoke whenever we wanted, in designated areas. Walking to the PX or from the chow hall was now also permitted. Conversation with others was not a mortal sin. All the military procedures that had been drilled into us were still very much alive. Standing at attention when talking to a DI and saluting an officer were second nature to us now.

Responsibilities were pretty much left up to the individual. It was our obligation to be prepared for the unexpected, since that was what our training was all about. Cleaning the barracks and our rifles and keeping our clothes in order were part of our daily routine. Inspections could be called for at any given moment, and we had to be prepared for them, whether it be rifle, clothing, or barracks inspection. Only this time if the person wasn't squared away, he was held accountable for himself, instead of the whole platoon being held responsible. That didn't happen very often. Platoon 2028 had arrived. May I say, with some reservation, that without Sergeant Grant it wouldn't have been that way. The feeling that I was now experiencing was a feeling of freedom, like being let out of prison. I can say one thing. If prison were like PI, there would be fewer repeat offenders.

One added privilege that we had been given was going to the PX. It was like a small supermarket on base. No food was sold with the exception of candy (poggy bait) or gum. Toilet articles, stationery, and other small items were sold. There was not an open book to go there; we had to get permission to go there as well as everywhere else. But we were no longer under a microscope.

Just about two weeks before we were to graduate, I got the scare of my life. For some unknown reason, I developed tonsillitis. I had had my tonsils removed when I was very young, but the tips of them now became inflamed. I was confined to sick bay for about three days. Carraffa came to see me. He told me he had heard that if I wasn't back with the platoon the next day, I was going to get sent back (and have to start boot camp over again). My heart almost stopped. A fate worse than death. I wasn't fully recovered but had enough penicillin in my to do the trick. I collected the gear I had brought with me and raced back to the barracks as fast as these skinny Italian legs could go. If I had to start boot camp all over again, I don't know what I would have done. I might have had to take an unauthorized swim through the swamps. When I got to the barracks, Sergeant Grant was standing in the middle of the squad bay. He looked at me, made some kind of face, turned around, and walked away. I never tried to interpret that look but was just happy to be back, thanks to my good friend Carraffa.

Chapter 28
Elliott's Beach

Through all of our training, discipline was the most important element we learned. Marching fifteen or twenty miles in full gear at a ninety-five-degree temperature required total discipline and conditioning.

Elliott's Beach was an area set up in the boondocks, probably named after a marine hero. The entire march out there was a cakewalk. Part of the time we ran; part of the time we marched. Along the way we sang the song that we had been taught by our headmaster cutting up the army and navy. We stopped once for a water break and a short rest period. No one complained; no one lagged behind. It was about time I didn't have to carry someone.

While at Elliott's Beach, we learned how to live in the woods, pitch tents, cook over open fires, purify drinking water, dig foxholes, set up temporary showers, perform first aid, and do anything else that was necessary to get by in the field. It was nice to learn something useful and not be screamed at in the process.

This was the first time we had the pleasure of tasting C rations. This food was canned and used for consumption in the field, either in time of war or on maneuvers. The dates stamped on some of the cans dated back to the 1940s. I couldn't imaging eating something that was eighteen years old. But when a person is hungry, he will eat anything. There were such delicacies as franks and beans, pork and beans, ham and beans, and beans and just about anything you could think of. There was beef stew and lasagna and spaghetti that would make any good Italian's skin crawl. The only things that were edible were the desserts. Pound cake, peaches, fruit cocktail, pears, and apple sauce were some of the items. Trading C rations was common among the troops. Some of the hill jacks were so used to eating bad food, they thought they were eating at the Ritz Carlton when they opened these cans. I traded everything I didn't like and ate all the desserts. I traded Private Wayne a can of beef stew and spaghetti for a can of peaches and pound cake. He thought he was getting the better deal. If I was desperate, I would mix two of the cans together and try to kill the taste. At times, the pork and beans mixed with pork and franks wasn't bad. By this time my taste buds were shot. Eating C rations was a prime example of the fact that if someone is hungry, he will eat anything. There was so much salt in the rations to keep them from spoiling that if one of the cans spilled on a glacier by accident, in no time there would be a lake. Heating up these delectable morsels was done with Sterno. I don't know if they were better hot or cold.

For the smokers, there was an extra-special treat: twenty-year-old cigarettes. The cigarettes were older than most of the people who were smoking them. The packages were green from age. The smokes on the inside were as brittle as Sergeant Grant's personality. But after our long abstinence from cigarettes, we would smoke anything.

There were about six cigarette brands in C rations. At that time, filtered cigarettes had not been marketed yet. The brands we had were Camels, Lucky Strikes, Pall Mall, Old Gold, and a couple others. In those days, there was little, if any, knowledge of smoking causing cancer. It was said if you smoked, it would stunt your growth. My reply was: "I had intended to be six foot three; I'll settle for six foot."

Quite a bit of the training at Elliott's Beach was in first

aid, which included dressing wounds, making tourniquets, learning to set broken bones, and making stretchers out of material available.

The final segment of our training was learning the Oriental art of judo in three easy lessons. Judo is an art that utilizes your opponent's forward motion and weight to his disadvantage, mostly by takedowns or throws. Strength and size are not big factors in judo but do help if the technique is applied properly. If applied properly, judo is a very good means of self-defense.

The judo instructor was out of the same egotistical mold as the rest of the hot dog instructors. The first thing he tried to do, when instruction began, was show the recruits how good they were. The guy that taught the pugil stick and this guy had to be related.

First, we learned how to fall properly. After ten minutes of intensive training, we spent the next half hour getting bounced off the mats by Mr. Macho Man. This time was no exception: I was the first one up. The guy bounced me all over the mat like I was a rag doll. The only thing I learned about judo at that point was that this guy knew how to break my back.

Following his demonstration on me, we began to try the throws using other recruits. All in all, after the exhibition, the training was very useful and effective. We spent most of one day learning different throws and takedowns.

Some of the defenses we learned were how to disarm a person with a club, gun, or knife.

The forced march back to main side was as easy as the march there. There was an air of pride that swept through the platoon; we finally looked and acted like marines. Everyone in the platoon was gung ho (filled with pride and enthusiasm).

147

Chapter 29
Final Field

Final field was other terminology for final inspection and preparation before graduation. This inspection was held outdoors, behind the barracks, on the parade field. It resembled a junk on the bunk, only outdoors on the ground. All of our field gear was laid out on the ground: helmets, bayonets, rifles, mess gear, first-aid kits, knapsacks, and shelter halves. As with our clothing issue, all the gear had to be spit and polished.

The inspection began with a rifle inspection. By this time, we had become very proficient with our best friends. We were able to do fancy maneuvers, like spinning and snapping the weapons into different positions. A well-executed rifle inspection was very impressive to watch. The rifle was brought to port arms, and the DI would snap the weapon out of the recruit's hands and twirl it around in different positions to inspect it. During the inspection, the recruit had to answer questions about the rifle nomenclature. If the rifle and the recruit passed the inspection, the weapon was snapped back in his hand and brought to order arms. The good old boys had done their jobs well. Everyone looked exceptional.

Chapter 30

Dress Uniform Issue

Up until now, the only uniforms we had were working uniforms, called dungarees. We were now issued khaki uniforms, which were warn in warm climates. The uniforms that were worn in colder climates were called greens. They were made out of heavier blanket-type material. Unless they were tailored, they were not very good-looking uniforms. The overcoat that was issued was called a horse blanket. If it got wet, two people had to carry it, it got so heavy. Two different kinds of covers were issued for liberty. One was a slender hat called a piss cutter. The other was a cumbersome thing called a barracks cover. The barracks cover had a leather brim in the front that had to be shined with shoe polish. The piss cutter was preferred by everyone, because it was more comfortable to wear and better-looking.

Dress blues were uniforms that were worn on special occasions and on special duty assignments. These uniforms were not a standard issue. I never owned a set. The powers that be at PI tried to impress the recruits' parents and make a few bucks by taking pictures of each recruit in this uniform. These pictures were sent home to the recruit's parents in hopes of subsidizing our penniless government, something most parents didn't know about the pictures of their kids in dress blues, everyone that took the pictures wore the same two or three jackets for their photos. The jackets were slit up the back and the closest size was put on the person whose picture was being taken by slipping their arms through the back of the jacket. Toilet paper was then stuffed in the back of the neck area to tighten up the collar—just one more shortcut that the government took to save the taxpayers' money. Someone viewing the picture had no idea that everyone was basically wearing the same jacket; they would think that all the recruits were issued dress blues. If a person wanted dress blues, he had to purchase them. That had to be the worst picture I have ever taken. When I got home from boot camp on leave, I saw the picture and threw it right in the garbage.

Chapter 31
The Final Touches

The remaining time left in boot camp was spent drilling, marching, and having a few inspections, but basically preparing for graduation day, a day that everyone had thought would never come. Each and every night I still was the recipient of the green wienie, either by hand or by weight. I think that the old boy Sergeant Grant was surprised I was still standing up to all the punishment.

All of the platoon's parents were invited to attend the graduation ceremony, but most didn't come. Either they couldn't afford to come or they were in no hurry to see the kids they had just gotten rid of. Who knows?

Boot camp was definitely an experience I was totally unprepared for, and one I'm glad I'll never have to go through again. I can say I was a better person and a bitter person as well, better for the unbelievable physical condition I was in and bitter for the mental and physical pounding I took. It was a hard but well-learned lesson. I now felt confident that I could handle almost any adverse situation that would confront me. The physical training at PI was second to none. The mental conditioning tactics the DIs used was comparable to brainwashing. There were different times I almost "broke" from the mental harassment, but I never gave in. I have something inbred in me that would not let Sergeant Grant be victorious. He won most of the battles, but I won the war.

The guys that wore the Smokey the Bear hats were professionals and did their jobs well. In my case, Sergeant Grant went way overboard in his training methods. I now had a bigger chip on my shoulder than when I went into boot camp. Afterwards I was much more capable of being destructive—and I didn't know if that was good or bad.

In retrospect, I think that boot camp needed to be as tough as it was in the '50s to produce the type of person the Marine Corps wanted. The push-ups and the sit-ups didn't bother me, it was the beatings I could have done without.

All of these experiences can be written and read about, but for someone to have the full impact of a Marine Corps boot camp and to understand what Sergeant Grant's special teaching techniques were like, he would have had to have lived it.

Chapter 32

The Final Chapter

Graduation day was a day everyone looked forward to that sometimes seemed an eternity away. Thirteen weeks at times seemed like thirteen years. Still, the last weeks of training were not as mentally intense as the beginning. I came here to be in the U.S. Marine Corps, and here I was, almost a marine.

When I arrived at PI I weighed 150 pounds. I was leaving weighing 186 pounds, and not one of the added pounds was fat. As the slogan goes, join the marines; they will make a man out of you. That they did. Just what kind is a different story. I received an education in boot camp that stayed with me the rest of my life. It had nothing to do with book knowledge, just how to cope when things got tough.

Two things stayed indelibly in my mind: Sergeant Grant's face and my serial number, 1830873. Was he a good teacher or a sadist? I think a combination of both. I know one thing for sure: I did a lot of bending, but in the long run I never broke.

The time we had all been waiting for finally came. The graduation ceremony was over faster than it began. As we marched passed the reviewing stand, the Marine Corps Hymn was played. To this day, I still get the chills when I hear that song.

Our seabags were packed and the buses were parked in front of the barracks to take us to Camp Geiger in North Carolina for advanced infantry training. The sun was out and it was a gorgeous day. The feeling I was experiencing was like that of someone getting released from Sing Sing (a maximum-security prison). One by one, the marines, not maggots anymore, boarded the buses. I got in the bus and took a window seat that was facing the barracks. I wanted one good look before I left. When I was seated, it felt like ten tons of weight were lifted off my shoulders. I let out a big sigh of relief.

As I looked out the window at the barracks, walking over to where the bus was parked was none other than Sergeant Grant. He looked through the window at me and in his very familiar voice called, "Private Iacampo, get your fuckin' ass off the bus and report to me on the double!" My heart almost stopped. I didn't know what to expect. Maybe he wanted to administer the green wienie to me once more for good luck. I didn't know. This guy wouldn't even let me leave in peace. I jumped up as I had done a thousand times before and ran down the aisle and off the bus. I stood at attention in front of him the same way I was used to and reported.

"SIR, PRIVATE IACAMPO IS REPORTING AS ORDERED, SIR."

He never cracked a smile. Looking at me nose to nose, toes to toes, and eyeball to eyeball, he said, "Private Iacampo, you will make a good fuckin' marine, if you can learn to keep that big fuckin' mouth of yours shut."

"SIR, YES SIR."

At that point, he stuck out his hand and shook hands with me but never cracked a smile. He didn't disappoint me.

"Now get the fuck out of here, boy."

"Sir, yes sir."

I did an about-face and ran for the bus.

It was finally over. I could say I had made it through Marine Corps boot camp. The hard way, but I made it. As the bus pulled away, I never looked back.